TERRORISM IN AFRICA: THE IMMINENT THREAT TO THE UNITED STATES

HEARING

BEFORE THE

SUBCOMMITTEE ON COUNTERTERRORISM AND INTELLIGENCE

OF THE

COMMITTEE ON HOMELAND SECURITY HOUSE OF REPRESENTATIVES

ONE HUNDRED FOURTEENTH CONGRESS

FIRST SESSION

APRIL 29, 2015

Serial No. 114–16

Printed for the use of the Committee on Homeland Security

Available via the World Wide Web: http://www.gpo.gov/fdsys/

U.S. GOVERNMENT PUBLISHING OFFICE

94–891 PDF

WASHINGTON : 2015

For sale by the Superintendent of Documents, U.S. Government Publishing Office
Internet: bookstore.gpo.gov   Phone: toll free (866) 512–1800; DC area (202) 512–1800
Fax: (202) 512–2104   Mail: Stop IDCC, Washington, DC 20402–0001

COMMITTEE ON HOMELAND SECURITY

MICHAEL T. MCCAUL, Texas, *Chairman*

LAMAR SMITH, Texas
PETER T. KING, New York
MIKE ROGERS, Alabama
CANDICE S. MILLER, Michigan, *Vice Chair*
JEFF DUNCAN, South Carolina
TOM MARINO, Pennsylvania
PATRICK MEEHAN, Pennsylvania
LOU BARLETTA, Pennsylvania
SCOTT PERRY, Pennsylvania
CURT CLAWSON, Florida
JOHN KATKO, New York
WILL HURD, Texas
EARL L. "BUDDY" CARTER, Georgia
MARK WALKER, North Carolina
BARRY LOUDERMILK, Georgia
MARTHA MCSALLY, Arizona
JOHN RATCLIFFE, Texas

BENNIE G. THOMPSON, Mississippi
LORETTA SANCHEZ, California
SHEILA JACKSON LEE, Texas
JAMES R. LANGEVIN, Rhode Island
BRIAN HIGGINS, New York
CEDRIC L. RICHMOND, Louisiana
WILLIAM R. KEATING, Massachusetts
DONALD M. PAYNE, JR., New Jersey
FILEMON VELA, Texas
BONNIE WATSON COLEMAN, New Jersey
KATHLEEN M. RICE, New York
NORMA J. TORRES, California

BRENDAN P. SHIELDS, *Staff Director*
JOAN V. O'HARA, *General Counsel*
MICHAEL S. TWINCHEK, *Chief Clerk*
I. LANIER AVANT, *Minority Staff Director*

SUBCOMMITTEE ON COUNTERTERRORISM AND INTELLIGENCE

PETER T. KING, New York, *Chairman*

CANDICE S. MILLER, Michigan
LOU BARLETTA, Pennsylvania
JOHN KATKO, New York
WILL HURD, Texas
MICHAEL T. MCCAUL, Texas *(ex officio)*

BRIAN HIGGINS, New York
WILLIAM R. KEATING, Massachusetts
FILEMON VELA, Texas
BENNIE G. THOMPSON, Mississippi *(ex officio)*

MANDY BOWERS, *Subcommittee Staff Director*
DENNIS TERRY, *Subcommittee Clerk*
HOPE GOINS, *Minority Subcommittee Staff Director*

CONTENTS

TERRORISM IN AFRICA: THE IMMINENT THREAT TO THE UNITED STATES

Wednesday, April 29, 2015

U.S. House of Representatives,
Committee on Homeland Security,
Subcommittee on Counterterrorism and Intelligence,
Washington, DC.

The subcommittee met, pursuant to call, at 12:22 p.m., in Room 311, Cannon House Office Building, Hon. Peter T. King [Chairman of the subcommittee] presiding.

Present: Representatives King, Barletta, Katko, Higgins, and Vela.

Also present: Representatives Jackson Lee and Wilson of Florida.

Mr. KING. The committee will come to order. Subcommittee on Counterterrorism and Intelligence will come to order. We are meeting today for our second hearing of the 114th Congress to hear testimony from three distinguished experts regarding terrorism in Africa and the imminent threat to the United States.

I would like to welcome the Members of the subcommittee, and my appreciation for the witnesses who are here today.

Now I will make an opening statement.

We understand there are going to be votes at about 1:15 or 1:20, so we will try to get through the opening statements, and then certainly we want to hear what you have to say. We thank you for being here today.

We are holding this hearing to raise awareness and to discuss threats related to the spread of Islamist terror ideology on the African continent. While this has been happening over the last decade, I still do not believe that the United States has an appropriate counterterrorism strategy to address the threat, which leaves the homeland and U.S. interests vulnerable.

There is no doubt that we are behind the curve in taking threats from terror groups in Africa seriously. We have seen on too many occasions that al-Qaeda-affiliated groups in Africa will attack American and Western interests when they see an opening. This was true in Libya, Algeria, Nigeria, and Kenya.

Documents received from bin Laden's Abbottabad compound show how the dead terror leader was looking for operatives in Africa to carry out Western attacks. We saw this materialize on December 25, 2009, when a Nigerian national, Abdulmutallab, was directed by al-Qaeda in the Arabian Peninsula to carry out an attack on a U.S.-bound plane.

Now we are seeing clear evidence of the Islamic State of Iraq and Syria, ISIS, seeking to expand partnerships with Islamist terror

(1)

groups in Africa. Boko Haram in Nigeria, terror groups in Egypt and Libya, and certain factions within al-Qaeda in the Islamic Maghreb have pledged allegiance to ISIS leadership. This does not lessen the threat these groups pose to the United States.

While it is imperative that the United States maintain and increase counterterrorism pressure in the Middle East and South Asia, we would be foolish to turn our backs on the imminent and growing threat posed by terror groups operating in Africa. The administration has not devoted, I believe, enough attention and resources to fight this growing threat.

Emboldened by the lack of consequences, Africa-based Islamist terrorist groups in recent months have perpetuated numerous acts of violence against innocent people. During Easter in Kenya al-Shabaab murdered hundreds of Christian students at a university. This was the same group of Islamist terrorist who slaughtered 67 men, women, and children at Nairobi's Westgate Mall in 2013.

In February of this year al-Shabaab, headquartered in Somalia, urged attacks on Western shopping malls, calling out the Mall of America in Minnesota by name.

In Nigeria—and I realize we have several members today who are sitting on the panel because of their special interest in Nigeria—even though all of us have an interest, they have particular interest—Boko Haram kidnapped 276 girls from a school and, it is widely believed by U.S. officials, sold them into slavery, prostitution, and forced marriages.

Now, I understand that the Nigerian military, perhaps, I think, in the last 24 hours, did rescue nearly 300 men—300 women and girls from Boko Haram terror camps, and this is extremely positive. If the report is true, all of us are gratified by that. However, there are still the original 200 who were kidnapped in 2014 are still missing.

In August 2011 this group claimed responsibility for a car bomb outside the U.N. headquarters killing more than 20 people. The State Department designated Boko Haram a foreign terrorist organization in November 2013. This was more than 2 years after the group conducted its first attack against a Western interest, and also long after a number of Members of this committee asked to have it declared a foreign terrorist organization.

Earlier this month the group publicly pledged allegiance to ISIS leadership, announced its new name as Islamic State's West African Province.

In Algeria and Mali, al-Qaeda in the Islamic Maghreb aims to overthrow the government of Algeria and begin its own Islamic caliphate. It has spawned splinter groups whose goal is to unite all Muslims from the Nile to the Atlantic in jihad against Westerners.

In Libya, ISIS may have control over as much as three provinces, in November of last year reportedly took over the city of Derna, a Mediterranean coastal town just across from the Greek island of Crete, a popular tourist destination for Westerners, including Americans, and not very far from the coasts of Sicily and Israel. In February ISIS released a video of the brutal execution of 21 Egyptian Christians kidnapped in Libya.

In addition, there are splinter groups and smaller sympathetic jihadist organizations in almost every North African nation. Africa is clearly a ripe recruiting ground for ISIS and al-Qaeda—one that both have shown all-too-happy to exploit.

Both ISIS and al-Qaeda are actively recruiting residents and citizens of Western nations, including the United States, to commit acts of jihad. We have been accustomed to hearing news of Americans or Brits arrested for joining or attempting to join ISIS or planning attacks in their home country.

The intelligence community, particularly the FBI, is to be commended for its proactive role in preventing these persons from achieving their violent aims. Yet, I still do not believe there is an overall strategy for dealing with this urgent threat at its source. I am concerned that as we improve our ability to prevent Americans and others from joining ISIS in Syria and Iraq, home-grown jihadists may seek training with affiliated groups in Africa.

As like-minded Islamic groups join forces and conquer new territory in Africa, it is time for the United States to treat every ounce of terrorism as the sobering threat it is, whether that source is in Syria or Somalia, in Mosul or Mozambique, in Tikrit or Tunisia. We have, therefore, invited a distinguished panel of experts to share their expertise with us on this terrorist threat from Africa and what the political leaders of the United States must do to protect our citizens and prevent a terrorist attack in the United States.

With that, I conclude my remarks and I recognize the distinguished Ranking Member, Mr. Higgins, from New York.

Mr. HIGGINS. I would like to thank the Chairman for holding this hearing today, and for the witnesses for their participation.

Violent Islamist extremists are not new in Africa. Al-Qaeda's bombing of the U.S. embassies in Kenya and Tanzania in 1998 demonstrate its reach and its ability to recruit from Africa's Muslim communities.

Groups in Algeria and Somalia later affiliated themselves with al-Qaeda. Foreign fighter flows from North and East Africa to Afghanistan and Iraq have long been of international concern, as are flows to Syria.

High-profile extremist attacks have intensified in recent years, including mass casualty bombings in Uganda, Nigeria, and Somalia; attacks on U.S. facilities in Benghazi and Tunis in 2012, and U.N. facilities in Algeria, Nigeria, and Somalia; deadly sieges at Algeria's major gas plant in Kenya's Westgate Mall in 2013; the 2014 abduction of more than 270 Nigerian school girls; executions of Christians in Libya; and the recent attack on Tunisia's Bardo Museum and a university in Kenya. These are a few examples of a growing list.

Specifically, al-Qaeda operatives and other violent extremists—Islamist extremist groups have had a presence in East Africa for 2 decades. In the 1990s Sudan hosted foreign extremists, including Osama bin Laden.

Al-Shabaab emerged in predominantly Muslim Somalia in the early 2000s, amid the proliferation of Islamists in clan-based militias that flourished in the absence of central government authority. Some of its founding members trained and fought with al-Qaeda in Afghanistan, and known al-Qaeda operatives were associated with the group during its founding.

Today, al-Shabaab continues to wage a violent campaign against the Somalia government, the African Union forces, and international targets in Somalia. Al-Shabaab activity in Kenya has also increased significantly in recent years. More than 600 people have been killed in attacks there since 2012.

Its leaders have issued repeated threats against the United States and Western targets in Somalia and beyond and have called for strikes against the United States. A February 2015 video from a group advocated attacks in Kenya and abroad and named several shopping malls in Europe and the United States as potential targets, including Minnesota's Mall of America.

On January 1, 2008 my neighbor and constituent, John Granville, and his advisor, Abdel Abbas, were killed while killed while promoting free and fair elections in South Sudan on behalf of the United States Agency for International Development. Mr. Granville and Mr. Abbas were killed by Islamic extremists after leaving the British Embassy on New Year's Eve.

Today, two of his killers are believed to be among al-Shabaab's ranks. I am still pushing the United States Department of State to pressure the government of Sudan to bring about justice for Mr. Granville and Mr. Abbas.

When we look at these kinds of attacks, it is important that we keep them in the proper context while remaining aware and vigilant.

I look forward to a robust discussion with the witnesses today about terrorist groups in Africa; their rivalries for resources, recruits, and territory; and how we can shape U.S. policy to counter their efforts.

I yield back.

[The statement of Ranking Member Higgins follows:]

STATEMENT OF RANKING MEMBER BRIAN HIGGINS

APRIL 29, 2015

Violent Islamist extremists in Africa are not a new phenomenon. Al-Qaeda's bombings of the U.S. embassies in Kenya and Tanzania in 1998 demonstrated its reach and ability to recruit from Africa's Muslim communities. Groups in Algeria and Somalia later affiliated themselves with al-Qaeda. Foreign fighter flows from North and East Africa to Afghanistan and Iraq have long been of international concern, as are flows to Syria.

High-profile extremist attacks have intensified in recent years, including mass casualty bombings in Uganda, Nigeria, and Somalia; attacks on U.S. facilities in Benghazi and Tunis in 2012 and U.N. facilities in Algeria, Nigeria, and Somalia; deadly sieges at Algeria's In Amenas gas plant and Kenya's Westgate Mall in 2013; the 2014 abduction of more than 270 Nigerian schoolgirls; executions of Christians in Libya; and the recent attacks on Tunisia's Bardo Museum and a university in Garissa, Kenya, among others.

Those are a few examples on a growing list. Specifically, al-Qaeda operatives and other violent Islamist extremist groups have had a presence in East Africa for 2 decades. In the 1990s, Sudan hosted foreign extremists, including Osama bin Laden.

Al-Shabaab emerged in predominately Muslim Somalia in the early 2000s amid a proliferation of Islamist and clan-based militias that flourished in the absence of central government authority. Some of its founding members trained and fought with al-Qaeda in Afghanistan, and known al-Qaeda operatives were associated with the group during its founding. Today, al-Shabaab continues to wage a violent campaign against the Somali government, AU forces, and international targets in Somalia.

Al-Shabaab activity in Kenya has also increased significantly in recent years; more than 600 people have been killed in its attacks there since 2012. Its leaders have issued repeated threats against U.S. and Western targets in Somalia and beyond, and have called for strikes against the United States. A February 2015 video from the group advocated attacks in Kenya and abroad, and named several shopping malls in Europe and the United States as potential targets, including Minnesota's Mall of America.

On January 1, 2008, my neighbor and constituent, John Granville and his driver, Abdel Rahman Abbas, were killed while promoting free and fair elections in South Sudan on behalf of the U.S. Agency for International Development (USAID). Mr. Granville and Mr. Abbas were killed by Islamic extremists after leaving the British Embassy. Today, two of his killers are believed to be among al-Shabaab's ranks. I am still pushing the U.S. Department of State to pressure the government of Sudan to bring about justice for Mr. Granville and Mr. Abbas.

When we look at these kinds of attacks it is important to keep them in the proper context, while remaining aware and vigilant. I look forward to a robust discussion with our witnesses today about terrorist groups in Africa, their rivalries for resources, recruits, and territory, and how we can shape U.S. policy to counter their efforts.

Mr. KING. I thank the Ranking Member, and I thank him and his staff for the cooperation they have shown in making this a truly bipartisan hearing. Other Members are reminded that statements may be submitted for the record.

[The statement of Ranking Member Thompson follows:]

STATEMENT OF RANKING MEMBER BENNIE G. THOMPSON

APRIL 29, 2015

Over the past 5 years, democracy and progress have been marching forward in Africa and the Middle East. These strides have made life more difficult for terrorist groups. The United States continues to engage in military and civilian efforts to counter violent extremism in Africa. While most of our military efforts have eliminated senior leadership within terrorist organizations, these missions have also killed civilians.

Perfection is not possible, but we must continue to ensure that our missions remain targeted and properly executed. As our interests and military actions become almost exclusively focused on the recent gains of the Islamic State, I would encourage my colleagues to remember that other terrorist groups remain active.

Prior to the Charlie Hebdo attacks in Paris earlier this year, al-Qaeda's operations appeared to have been diminished. However, it seems that now, perhaps in response to our growing interest in the Islamic State, al-Qaeda is intent on reminding us that it remains a threat to the United States. Today, we will hear testimony to confirm that while the methods may be different, the end-game for the groups within Africa is the same, whether they remain independent or pledge allegiance to a more established terrorist organization.

For example, Boko Haram has now pledged its allegiance to the Islamic State. Boko Haram is responsible for killing over 11,000 people, including more than 5,000 this year alone. Until recently, the out-going president of Nigeria did not seem equipped or ready to effectively fight Boko Haram. Boko Haram's focus on targeting women and children, including the kidnapping of over 200 school girls last April, garnered international attention and spawned the social media campaign "Bring Back Our Girls."

Yesterday, after a full year of military and civilian pressure from Nigerian officials and international partners, including the United States, 200 girls were rescued from a Boko Haram camp by the Nigerian army. We do not know for sure if these are the same girls that were kidnapped last April, but we do know that Boko Haram forcibly uses women and girls as sex slaves and fighters. The rescue of these girls is nothing short of miraculous, but more needs to be done to diminish the capabilities of Boko Haram. I am hopeful that with Nigeria's change in leadership and international cooperation, substantive strides can be made against Boko Haram.

No matter where these terrorist groups are located, all of them remain united in their goals to cause devastation in the United States and abroad. In order for us to wage an effective assault against the Islamic State and al-Qaeda, it is important for us to review what has worked in the past.

However, I would again warn that hearings like this may incite panic among the public without immediate and imminent threats. As capabilities diminish in groups like al-Qaeda and the Islamic State, they will begin to use our fears as their propaganda. I want to be clear. I am not advocating ignoring credible threats and standing in the face of danger. Credible threats cannot be ignored. But what also cannot be ignored are the costs of terrorism and terrorist threats. The methods currently used to decrease the reach and presence of terrorist organizations have limits that must be exercised when there is no credible and actionable intelligence.

Mr. KING. Now, without objection, I would ask unanimous consent for Ms. Wilson to sit at the dais and participate in the hearing.

Hearing no objections, so ordered.

Our first panelist this morning is Dr. J. Peter Pham, who is the director of the Atlantic Council's Africa Center. He was previously senior vice president of the National Committee on American Foreign Policy and editor of its bimonthly journal, American Foreign Policy Interests.

He was also a tenured associate professor at James Madison University, where he was director of the Nelson Institute for International and Public Affairs. He has served on the senior advisory group of the U.S. Africa Command since its creation.

Dr. Pham.

STATEMENT OF J. PETER PHAM, DIRECTOR, AFRICA CENTER, ATLANTIC COUNCIL

Mr. PHAM. Thank you very much, Mr. Chairman.

I would like to present a summary of my prepared remarks and ask that the entirety be entered into the record.

Mr. KING. Without objection.

Mr. PHAM. Thank you.

Mr. Chairman, Ranking Member Higgins, distinguished Members of the subcommittee, Ms. Wilson, I would like to begin by thanking you not only for the specific opportunity to testify today on the subject of terrorism in Africa, but also thank you for the sustained attention that the United States House of Representatives has in general given to this challenge.

I failed to recall that it was this Subcommittee on Counterterrorism and Intelligence that in 2011 convened the very first Congressional hearing on Boko Haram. At that time, Boko Haram was considered so obscure that all the participants at that event could have assembled in the proverbial broom closet.

Sadly, our analysis proved prescient and, rather than fading away as some dismissively suggested that it would, Boko Haram went on to pose an even greater menace—not only to Nigeria and its people, but to their neighbors in West Africa as well as international security writ large.

There is a recurring trope that emerges time and time again about terrorism in Africa: It generally gets short shrift and, when attention is focused on specific groups or situations that appear to be emerging challenges, the threat is either dismissed entirely or minimized until tragedy strikes. Yet, dating back to at least the period when Osama bin Laden himself found refuge in Sudan, the leading strategists of Islamist terrorism have speculated about the potential opportunities to establish cells, recruit members, obtain financing, and find safe haven offered by the weak governance capacities and other vulnerabilities of African states.

At present there are four geographic areas of particular concern in Africa with respect to terrorist groups and their activities: North

Africa, the Sahel, Nigeria, and East Africa, as well as emerging challenges.

In North Africa, the Maghreb is home to some cf the longest-running terrorist campaigns on the African continent. More recently, however, the mix has become all the more combustible with the emergence of three so-called provinces aligned with the Islamic State in Iraq and the Levant amid the disintegration of Libya, alongside with preexisting groups like al-Qaeda in the Islamic Maghreb, as well as others, which emerged in the wake of the collapse of the Muammar Gaddafi regime.

As you noted, Mr. Chairman, the brutal murder in February of 20 Coptic Christians from Egypt along with a Christian from Ghana by the Islamic State's Libyan cohorts, as well as the execution this month of approximately 30 Ethiopian Christians, highlights the malevolence of the witch's brew that has been allowed to simmer on the very shores of the Mediterranean Sea, close to the vital, but narrow sea lanes as well as to Europe itself.

In the Sahel, in many respects that belt connecting North Africa and West Africa, stretching from the Atlantic to the Red Sea, is very much a transnational challenge. Not only has it been a conduit for arms, fighters, and ideologies back and forth across the Sahara, but it has emerged as a battle space in its own right.

Nigeria: While the West African giant, Africa's most populous country and biggest economy, has demonstrated over the decades a legendary resilience, the reemergence in 2010 of Boko Haram and its increasing virulence, reflecting major transformations in capacity, tactics, and ideology, are nonetheless a cause for concern, not least because the attacks last year alone left more than 10,000 people dead across northern and central Nigeria and displaced at least 1.5 million others.

In the short period of just under 5 years, Boko Haram has gone from a small militant group focused on localized concerns to a major insurgency, seizing and holding large swaths of territory. More recently, it has even started another shift with the pledge of allegiance to the so-called Islamic State.

In East Africa, although the adoption of effective counterinsurgency strategy by the more recent commanders of the African Union force, as well as Shabaab's own blunders, has led the group to become gradually pushed out of Mogadishu and other urban centers, it—Shabaab remains a primary terrorist threat in the region. In fact, the attack on the Westgate Mall in Nairobi in 2013, which killed 67 people, as was noted, and the attack at the beginning of this month at Garissa University College, which left 148 victims dead and 79 wounded, are just the most notorious assaults by Shabaab.

Moreover, the better-known terrorist groups mentioned are by far not the only ones out of Africa that should be of concern. In fact, as past experience has shown, emergent challenges call out for even greater attention precisely because they are poorly known, much less understood, and as nevertheless can be seen, can evolve very quickly.

Let me summarize by pointing to six areas where I think U.S. policy needs to work.

First, time and again the mistake has been made to underestimate, if not discount entirely, the threat faced. Part of this is attributable to analytical bias to limit future possibilities to extrapolations from the past. Another part is more basic: The sheer lack of resources for Africa-related intelligence and analysis.

Second, with the exception of the Department of Defense with the U.S. Africa Command, across the U.S. Government there is an artificial division of the continent, which, quite frankly, is rejected not only by Africans, but unhelpful.

Third, USAFRICOM, since its establishment, has been hampered by less-than-adequate resources.

Fourth, closely related to terrorism is the danger posed by lack of effective sovereignty that bedevils African governments, and that requires assistance to build up those capabilities.

Fifth, America's relationships—diplomatic, security, economic, and cultural—with Africa as a whole, and individual countries on the continent, expand and deepen—a positive development, to be sure—an unfortunate downside is the potential risk to U.S. persons and interests as well as the homeland necessarily increases. Quite simply, the threats are there and, by their very nature, more engagement means exposure and vulnerability.

Sixth and finally, the challenge of terrorism in Africa and any derivative threat to the United States cannot be addressed except in an integrated fashion.

Mr. Chairman, I thank you and the Members of the subcommittee for your attention. I look forward to your questions.

Thank you.

[The prepared statement of Mr. Pham follows:]

PREPARED STATEMENT OF J. PETER PHAM

APRIL 29, 2015

Mr. Chairman, Ranking Member Higgins, distinguished Members of the subcommittee: I would like to begin by thanking you not only for the specific opportunity to testify before you today on the subject of terrorism in Africa, but also for the sustained attention the United States House of Representatives has, in general, given to this challenge. In its oversight capacity, the House has been very much ahead of the curve over the course of the last decade-and-half and it has been my singular privilege to have contributed, however modestly, to the effort.

It was at a 2005 briefing organized by the Subcommittee on International Terrorism and Nonproliferation of the then-Committee on International Relations, that al-Shabaab was first mentioned as a threat not only to the security of Somalia, but also to the wider East Africa region and, indeed, the United States.

The following spring, a joint hearing of the same Subcommittee on International Terrorism and Nonproliferation and the Subcommittee on Africa, Global Human Rights, and International Operations first raised the alarm about the expanding crisis in the Horn of Africa occasioned by the takeover of Somalia by Islamist forces, including al-Shabaab.

And, of course, it was this esteemed Subcommittee on Intelligence and Counterterrorism of the Committee on Homeland Security that, in 2011, convened the very first Congressional hearing on Boko Haram in 2011, at which I also had the privilege of testifying. At that time, Boko Haram was considered so obscure that the all the participants at the event, held in conjunction with the release of a bipartisan report spearheaded by Representatives Patrick Meehan and Jackie Speier on the threat posed by the militant group, could have convened in the proverbial broom closet. Sadly, our analysis proved prescient and, rather than fading away as some dismissively suggested that it would, Boko Haram went on to pose an even greater menace, not only to Nigeria and its people, but to their neighbors in West Africa as well as to international security writ large.

In each of these cases and, indeed, others that could be cited, there is a recurring trope that emerges time and again: Terrorism in Africa generally gets short shrift and, when attention is focused on specific groups or situations that appear to be emerging challenges, the threat is either dismissed entirely or minimized—until tragedy strikes. Thus the Congress and the American people were assured 10 years ago by the "conventional wisdom" of experts, both inside and outside government, that the Union of Islamic Courts, of which al-Shabaab was the armed wing, was a "law-and-order" group; similarly, 5 years ago the same analysts were virtually unanimous in their conviction that al-Qaeda in the Islamic Maghreb (AQIM) was more of a criminal racket than a "real" terrorist organization; and, in this very room less than 4 years ago, this panel was told by some witnesses that Boko Haram was some sort of misunderstood social-justice movement that should not be put on the foreign terrorist organization list.

BACKGROUND ON TERRORISM IN AFRICA

It is worth recalling that Africa had been a theater for terrorist operations, including those directed against the United States, long before the attacks of September 11, 2001, on the homeland focused attention on what had hitherto been regions seemingly peripheral to the strategic landscape, at least as most American policymakers and analysts perceived it. In 1973, Palestine Liberation Organization terrorists acting on orders from Yasir Arafat murdered U.S. Ambassador to Sudan Cleo A. Noel, Jr., and his deputy, George Curtis Moore, as well as the Belgian chargé d'affaires and two Saudi diplomats. In 1998, there were the coordinated bombings of the U.S. embassies in Dar es Salaam, Tanzania, and Nairobi, Kenya, which killed 224 people—including 12 Americans—and wounded some 5,000 others. And these were just the more notorious acts of *international terrorism*. If one takes as a definition of terrorism the broadly accepted description offered by the United Nations General Assembly 1 year after the East Africa bombings—"criminal acts intended or calculated to provoke a state of terror in the general public, a group of persons or particular persons for political purposes"—terrorism can be said to be widespread in Africa, although it has largely been a domestic, rather than transnational, affair. However, just because the majority of actors and the incidents they are responsible for are domestic to African countries does not mean that they cannot and do not evolve into international threats when, in fact, that is the trajectory many, if not most, aspire to and which quite a few have indeed succeeded in achieving.

The first post-9/11 iteration of the *National Security Strategy of the United States of America*, released a year after the attacks on the American homeland, raised the specter that "weak states . . . can pose as great a danger to our national interests as strong states. Poverty does not make poor people into terrorists and murderers. Yet poverty, weak institutions, and corruption can make weak states vulnerable to terrorist networks and drug cartels within their borders" (The White House 2002).[1] Extremism, however, requires opportunity if it is to translate radical intentionality into terrorist effect. A decade ago, one leading African security analyst succinctly summarized the situation in the following manner:

"The opportunity targets presented by peacekeepers, aid and humanitarian workers, donors and Western NGOs active in the continent are lucrative targets of subnational terrorism and international terrorism. Africa is also replete with potentially much higher value targets ranging from the massive oil investments (often by U.S. companies) in the Gulf of Guinea to the burgeoning tourist industry in South Africa."[2]

Thus there is a very real terrorist risk to U.S. persons and interests—a risk that is increasing with time if one looks at its three constituent elements: Threat, the

[1] The most recent iteration of the *National Security Strategy of the United States of America*, released February 6, 2015, couched the country's strategic objectives in Africa largely in terms of broader development goals, rather than traditional security concerns which were emphasized in earlier documents: "Africa is rising. Many countries in Africa are making steady progress in growing their economies, improving democratic governance and rule of law, and supporting human rights and basic freedoms. Urbanization and a burgeoning youth population are changing the region's demographics, and young people are increasingly making their voices heard. But there are still many countries where the transition to democracy is uneven and slow with some leaders clinging to power. Corruption is endemic and public health systems are broken in too many places. And too many governments are responding to the expansion of civil society and free press by passing laws and adopting policies that erode that progress. On-going conflicts in Sudan, South Sudan, the Democratic Republic of the Congo, and the Central African Republic, as well as violent extremists fighting governments in Somalia, Nigeria, and across the Sahel all pose threats to innocent civilians, regional stability, and our national security."
[2] Jakkie Cilliers, "Terrorism and Africa," *African Security Review* 12, no. 4 (2003): 100.

frequency or likelihood of adverse events; vulnerability, the likelihood of success of a particular threat category against a particular target; and cost, the total impact of a particular threat experienced by a vulnerable target, including both the "hard costs" of actual damages and the "soft costs" to production, the markets, etc. In short, the combination of these three factors—threat, vulnerability, and cost—raises considerably the overall risk assessment in Africa.

And this point is not lost upon those who wish us harm. Dating back to at least the period when Osama bin Laden himself found refuge in Sudan, the leading strategists of Islamist terrorism have speculated about the potential opportunities to establish cells, recruit members, obtain financing, and find safe haven offered by the weak governance capacities and other vulnerabilities of African states. In fact, it has been noted that al-Qaeda's first act against the United States came several years before the embassy bombings when it attempted to insert itself in the fight against the American-led humanitarian mission in Somalia. Moreover, one of the most systematic expositions of the particular allure of the continent to terrorists came from al-Qaeda's on-line magazine, *Sada al-Jihad* ("Echo of Jihad"). The June 2006 issue of that publication featured an article by one Abu Azzam al-Ansari entitled "Al-Qaeda is Moving to Africa," in which the author asserted:

"There is no doubt that al-Qaeda and the holy warriors appreciate the significance of the African regions for the military campaigns against the Crusaders. Many people sense that this continent has not yet found its proper and expected role and the next stages of the conflict will see Africa as the battlefield."

With a certain analytical rigor, Abu Azzam then proceeded to enumerate and evaluate what he perceived to be significant advantages to al-Qaeda shifting terrorist operations to Africa, including: The fact that jihadist doctrines have already been spread within the Muslim communities of many African countries; the political and military weakness of African governments; the wide availability of weapons; the geographical position of Africa vis-á-vis international trade routes; the proximity to old conflicts against "Jews and Crusaders" in the Middle East as well as new ones like Darfur, where the author almost gleefully welcomed the possibility of Western intervention; the poverty of Africa which "will enable the holy warriors to provide some finance and welfare, thus, posting there some of their influential operatives"; the technical and scientific skills that potential African recruits would bring to the jihadist cause; the presence of large Muslim communities, including ones already embroiled conflict with Christians or adherents of traditional African religions; the links to Europe through North Africa "which facilitates the move from there to carry out attacks"; and the fact that Africa has a wealth of natural resources, including hydrocarbons and other raw materials, which are "very useful for the holy warriors in the intermediate and long term." Abu Azzam concluded his assessment by sounding an ominous note:

"In general, this continent has an immense significance. Whoever looks at Africa can see that it does not enjoy the interest, efforts, and activity it deserves in the war against the Crusaders. This is a continent with many potential advantages and exploiting this potential will greatly advance the jihad. It will promote achieving the expected targets of Jihad. Africa is a fertile soil for the advance of jihad and the *jihadi* cause."

In retrospect, it was clearly a mistake for many to have dismissed Abu Azzam's analysis as devoid of operational effect. Shortly before the publication of the article, the Islamic Courts Union, an Islamist movement whose leaders included a number of figures linked to al-Qaeda, seized control of the sometime Somali capital of Mogadishu and subsequently overran most of the country. While intervention by neighboring Ethiopia in late December 2006 dislodged the Islamists, Somalia's internationally-recognized but otherwise ineffective "Transitional Federal Government" failed to make much headway in the face of a burgeoning insurgency spearheaded by al-Shabaab, which started out as an armed wing of the Islamic Courts. Until very recently, al-Shabaab dominated wide swathes of Somali territory and operated more or less freely in other areas not under their *de facto* control—with the exception of the autonomous Somaliland and Puntland regions in the north. And despite the setbacks that it has suffered in more recent times in terms of territorial losses to the internationally-backed African Union Mission in Somalia (AMISOM) and leaders eliminated by U.S. air strikes or Special Operations Forces, al-Shabaab nonetheless was formally accepted by Osama bin Laden's successor Ayman al-Zawahiri as an affiliate of al-Qaeda in 2012 and, as the horrific attack on Garissa University College in Kenya earlier this month reminded us, is still very much a lethal force to be reckoned with.

Another al-Qaeda ''franchise'' has sought to reignite conflict in Algeria and spread it to the Sahel, the critical boundary region where Sub-Saharan Africa meets North Africa and where vast empty spaces and highly permeable borders are readily exploitable by local and international militants alike both as a base for recruitment and training and as a conduit for the movement of personnel and materiel. In 2006, after years of decline during which they had been squeezed by intense pressure from the outside while beset by defections from within, members of the Salafist Group for Preaching and Combat (known by its French acronym, GSPC) formally pledged allegiance to Osama bin Laden and al-Qaeda and began identifying themselves in communiqués as ''Al-Qaeda Organization in the Islamic Maghreb'' (AQIM). Following its ''rebranding'' as an affiliate of al-Qaeda in 2006, AQIM expanded southward from Algeria, using the prestige of its new association to recruit ''a considerable number of Mauritanians, Libyans, Moroccans, Tunisians, Malians, and Nigerians,'' as its emir bragged in a 2008 interview he gave to the *New York Times*. AQIM's shift beyond the limits of its Algerian origins proved not just a geographical move, but also an operational transformation, with the group acquiring both new tactics and new allies to implement them. Evidence subsequently emerged of AQIM's increasing involvement in the burgeoning drug traffic transiting the group's new operational areas in the Sahel, in addition to its well-honed kidnappings for ransoms.

The potential for the Sahel region being the setting for an explosive mix of Islamist terrorism, secular grievances, and criminality was underscored in early 2012 in Mali. What started as a rebellion by the disaffected Tuareg population led to the overthrow of state authority in the country's three northernmost provinces with a combined territory the size of France and, following the marginalization of the ethnic separatists by their erstwhile Islamist partners, the entire area falling under the sway of AQIM and several allied groups. Only a timely French-led military intervention in early 2013 forestalled the total collapse of the Malian state, although again, the situation remains fragile as the suicide attack just 10 days ago on United Nations peacekeepers, which left at least a dozen people dead, underscored.

And while transnational terrorist challenges have been the preoccupation of America's policymakers, intelligence analysts, and military planners, most African governments are more concerned with the threat of ''domestic terrorism,'' cases which rarely receive much attention in the Western media.[3] The emphasis is less on transnational phenomena and more on acts confined within national boundaries and involving neither targets abroad nor foreign agents. Consequently, lack of both government capacity and social and economic opportunity, on top of political, ethnic, and religious tensions, makes many in Africa potential candidates for radicalization.

CURRENT TERRORIST THREATS

At present, there are four geographical areas of particular concern in Africa with respect to terrorist groups and their activities: North Africa, the Sahel, Nigeria, and East Africa. Having already discussed the first two areas, I will concentrate primarily on the second two as well as mention some emerging concerns.

North Africa.—The Maghreb is home to some of the longest-running terrorist campaigns on the African continent. More recently, however, the mix has become all the more combustible with the emergence of three ''provinces'' aligned with the so-called Islamic State in Iraq and the Levant (ISIL) amid the disintegration of Libya, alongside preexisting groups like AQIM and others like *Ansar al-Sharia* (''Partisans of Islamic Law'') which emerged in the wake of the collapse of the Muammar Gaddafi regime and took part in the September 2012 attack on the U.S. diplomatic compound in Benghazi, Libya, that killed U.S. Ambassador J. Christopher Stevens and three other American diplomatic and intelligence officials. The brutal murder in February of 20 Coptic Christians from Egypt along with a Christian from Ghana by ISIL's Libyan cohorts as well as the execution this month of approximately 30

---

[3] Most African states are parties to the former Organization of African Unity's 1999 Convention on the Prevention and Combating of Terrorism which defines ''terrorism'' as: ''Any act which is a violation of the criminal laws of a State Party and which may endanger the life, physical integrity or freedom of, or cause serious injury or death to, any person, any number of group of persons or causes or may cause damage to public or private property, natural resources, environmental or cultural heritage and is calculated to: (i) Intimidate, put in fear, force, coerce or induce any government, body, institution, the general public or any segment thereof, to do or to abstain from doing any act, or to adopt or abandon a particular standpoint, or to act according to certain principles; or (ii) disrupt any public service, the delivery of any essential service to the public or to create a public emergency; or (iii) create a general insurrection in a State'' (art. 1 § 3a).

Ethiopian Christians highlights the malevolence of the witch's brew that has been allowed to simmer in the region. In addition, the videography of the slaughter of the Christians on the very shores of the Mediterranean Sea only emphasizes—as, no doubt, the terrorists intended—the threat posed not only to the vital, but narrow, sea lanes, but the proximity of the violence to Europe itself.

Fortunately, commensurate with the challenges in this region, the international community also has solid allies with which to work on not just combatting terrorism, but countering its extremist roots. Notable among these partners is Morocco, whose aggressive, multi-pronged approach has much to commend it as does the kingdom's efforts to assist other countries in North and West Africa to fight radicalization. The signing during last year's U.S.-Africa Leaders Summit of a U.S.-Morocco Framework for Cooperation aimed at developing Moroccan training experts as well as jointly training civilian security and counterterrorism forces with other partners in the Maghreb and the Sahel recognizes the potential of this "triangular" approach.

The Sahel.—In many respects, the belt connecting North Africa and West Africa, stretching from the Atlantic Ocean to the Red Sea and straddling ancient trade and migration routes, is an ideal environment for extremist groups with transnational ambitions. The region is strategically important for several reasons, including its role as a bridge between the Arab Maghreb and black Sub-Saharan Africa as well as its important natural resources, both renewable and nonrenewable. Moreover, the Sahel touches several countries—including Algeria, Nigeria, and Sudan—with serious security challenges of their own that could easily spill over their borders. In fact, some scholars have argued that the Sahara and the Sahel form "a single space of movement" which, for purposes of the geography of terrorism, "should be considered as a continuum, something that the territorial approach of states and geopolitics prevents us from understanding"[4]—a point which policymakers and analysts would do well to take to heart.

In point of fact, not only has the Sahel been the conduit for arms, fighters, and ideologies flowing back and forth across the Sahara, but it has emerged as a battlespace in its own right with the takeover of northern Mali in 2012 and the ongoing fight against Islamist militants there as well as in Mauritania, Niger, and back into southern Libya. A number of international figures, not least United Nations Secretary-General Ban Ki-moon, have underscored that that "the rise of instability and insecurity in and around the Sahel" and the risk of "spillover" from the fighting in Mali could turn some of the region's "frozen conflicts" like the dispute over the Western Sahara into a "ticking time bomb."[5] In fact, crossovers between groups like the separatist Polisario Front and terrorist groups have already been witnessed during recent conflicts in the region, such as in the instances of the former providing AQIM's allies in northern Mali with both fighters and, in one notorious case, an Italian and two Spanish hostages to trade for ransom. Moreover, at the end of 2013, the U.S. State Department was declaring that the merger of Mokhtar Belmokhtar's AQIM splinter group, the *al-Mulathamun* ("those who sign in blood") Battalion, with MUJAO to form a new group, *al-Murabitoun* ("people of the garrison"), constituted "the greatest near-term threat to U.S. and Western interests"[6] in the region.

Nigeria.—While the West African giant has demonstrated over the decades an almost legendary capacity to absorb violence, the reemergence in 2010 of the militant group Boko Haram ("Western education is forbidden") and its increasing virulence—reflecting major transformations in capacity, tactics, and ideology—has nonetheless been a cause for concern, not least because its attacks last year alone left more than 10,000 people dead across northern and central Nigeria and displaced at least 1.5 million others. Nevertheless, in that short period of just under 5 years, Boko Haram has gone from a small militant group focused on localized concerns and using relatively low levels of violence to a significant terrorist organization with a clearer jihadist ideology to a major insurgency seizing and holding large swathes of territory. More recently, it even started what might well be another shift with its pledge of allegiance to the so-called Islamic State, although the result of this latest evolution is not altogether clear given the success to date of the on-going military campaign launched in early 2015 against the group by the Nigerian armed forces and their regional partners.

---

[4] Olivier Walther and Denis Retaille, *Sahara or Sahel? The Fuzzy Geography of Terrorism in West Africa* (Luxembourg: CEPS/INSTEAD, 2010), 11.
[5] United Nations Secretary-General Ban Ki-moon, quoted in Tim Witcher, "Ban says Western Sahara Risks being Drawn into Mali War," *Agence France-Presse*, April 9, 2013.
[6] U.S. Department of State, Office of the Spokesperson, Terrorist Designation of the al-Mulathamun Battalion, December 18, 2013.

Boko Haram's merger with the so-called Islamic State does not appear have much immediate impact on the battlefield. The different social and political contexts in which each operates and the vast geographical distance separating the two groups means that each will have to face its foes with little more than moral support from each other, notwithstanding some evidence of collaboration in cyberspace and in terms of media production. And, in fact, in the 2 weeks after it was accepted into the Islamic State's fold, Boko Haram, or Wilāyat al Sūdan al Gharbī ("[Islamic State] Province in the Land of the Blacks") or the "Islamic State West Africa Province" (ISWAP) as it started to style itself, lost control of most of the towns and other areas that it was holding, with Gwoza, the headquarters of Abubakar Shekau's aspiring Islamic state, being retaken by Nigerian troops on the very eve of the country's national elections.

Of course, Boko Haram's affiliation with ISIL could lead to the internationalization of a threat that has up to now largely been confined geographically. There is the risk that fighters from North Africa and other areas finding it harder to migrate to the self-proclaimed caliphate's territory in the Levant, may well choose to move to the Boko Haram emirate instead. ISIL spokesman Abu Mohammad al-Adnani, in his communiqué accepting the Nigerian group's allegiance on behalf of his leader, said as much, telling Muslims who could not get to Syria or Iraq that "a new door for you to migrate to the land of Islam and fight" had opened in Africa. In fact, the international support recently pouring in for the multinational African anti-Boko Haram force from the United States, France, the United Kingdom, and others may render the Nigerian militants' fight all the more attractive to these aspiring foreign jihadists. On the other hand, Boko Haram's success as a movement has largely been the result of its denunciations of the Nigerian political elites resonating with many ordinary citizens as well as its ethnic appeal to the Kanuri population in particular, both of which advantages could be lost if it becomes merely another "province" of a far-flung "Islamic State" focused on a broader jihadist agenda.

Another possible course of evolution for Boko Haram is also hinted at by ISIL's Dabiq publication in its special issue, published just this month, heralding the allegiance of the Nigerian group. In the issue, whose cover was emblazoned with the headline "Shari'ah Alone Will Rule Africa," the announcement of the tidings contained multiple references to "Christians" being "terrorized" and "captured and enslaved" by Boko Haram and allegations that Nigeria's "large population of hostile crusaders" had "not shied away from massacring the Muslims of West Africa"—rhetoric aimed at stoking conflict along sectarian lines. It certainly points to a possible new operational emphasis for a militarily weakened militant group.

East Africa.—East Africa has been not only a region which hosted Osama bin Laden and the then still-nascent al-Qaeda in the early 1990s, but also the setting for the 1998 bombings of the U.S. embassies in Dar es Salaam and Nairobi as well as of an Israeli-owned hotel in Mombasa, Kenya, and, simultaneously, a near-miss attack on an Israeli commercial airliner in 2002—all carried out by the terrorist network. But it is Somalia's al-Shabaab which has been the primary terrorist threat in the region. Founded in large part due to the efforts of Aden Hashi Ayro, a militant who had trained with al-Qaeda in Afghanistan in the 1990s, al-Shabaab began its existence as one of several armed wings of an Islamist movement, the Islamic Courts Union, which gradually gained control over most of southern and central Somalia in early 2006. Following the rout of the Islamic Courts Union by an Ethiopian military intervention in early 2007, al-Shabaab emerged as the spearhead of the internationally-supported Transitional Federal Government (TFG), which was then installed in Mogadishu for the first time.

Benefiting from the TFG's lack of legitimacy and general incompetence and corruption, al-Shabaab eventually managed to seize control of large sections of southern and central Somalia, including parts of Mogadishu, where it installed a brutal Islamist regime that, to the horror of many Somalis, carried out a number of harsh punishments on alleged malefactors even as it set up multi-million dollar rackets. Over time, the group has shifted its emphasis from a purely local focus on driving out foreign forces—first the Ethiopians and, subsequently, the AMISOM force propping up the TFG—to an increasingly transnational agenda, as evidenced both by its rhetoric and by a twin bombing in Kampala, Uganda, in July 2010, during the FIFA World Cup final match, which left 74 people dead and scores injured.

The adoption of an effective counterinsurgency strategy by more recent commanders of the African Union force as well as al-Shabaab's own blunders have, since the beginning of 2011, led to the group being gradually pushed out of Mogadishu, Kismayo, and other urban centers it long held. Consequently, al-Shabaab shifted its focus, with its long-standing formal proclamations of its adhesion to al-Qaeda being accepted by bin Laden's successor, who enrolled it as a formal affiliate in early 2012. With the Kenyan military intervention in Somalia in late

2011—itself a response to cross-border raids by Somali militants—and increasing ethnic and religious tensions within the former country between the ethnic Somalis and other largely Muslim minorities and larger, predominantly Christian, population groups, there is increasing risk of al-Shabaab capitalizing on the disaffection to gain greater entrée than it already enjoys. In fact, the attack on the Westgate shopping mall in Nairobi, Kenya, in September 2013, which killed 67 people and wounded nearly 200 others, and the attack at the beginning of this month on Garissa University College, which left 148 victims dead and 79 wounded, were just the most notorious assaults by al-Shabaab. Between the two attacks, the terrorists have been responsible for at least 60 attacks in just Kenya alone.

Thus, while the group has suffered significant setbacks as a military force as well as lost a number of its leaders to U.S. strikes—including its emir, Ahmed Abdi Godane, a.k.a. Muhktar Abu Zubair, last September, and its head of clandestine operations outside Somalia, Adnan Garaar, who was thought responsible for the Westgate attack, just a few weeks ago—it remains very much a serious threat to regional and international security, and perhaps, ironically, even more so since it is rapidly transforming into a full-fledged terrorist organization. This last point is especially troublesome for two reasons. First, after Somalis from Somalia and ethnic Somalis from outside Somalia, the two largest demographic groups within al-Shabaab are Kenyans who are not ethnically Somali and Tanzanians—thus highlighting the threat to the East Africa region. Second, if al-Shabaab is transmogrifying into a ''generic'' global jihadist organization, rather than an extremist group focused on Somalia, it does so with an advantage that other such groups do not have: A proven network (however small and minority within the larger community) of supporters in Europe and North America, as evidenced by the number of prosecutions and convictions obtained by Federal authorities of those found to be providing it with material support from this country—as well as by the incitement of current al-Shabaab leader Ahmed Umar, a.k.a. Abu Ubaidah, to attack the Mall of America and other shopping centers.

Emerging Challenges.—The better-known terrorist threats mentioned so far are not the only ones out of Africa that should be of concern; in fact, as past experience has shown, emergent challenges call out for perhaps even greater attention precisely because they are so poorly known, much less understood, but nevertheless can, as has been seen, evolve very quickly.

One example of such a group is the Allied Democratic Forces (ADF), which has operated in the borderlands between Uganda and the Democratic Republic of the Congo since the 1990s and shown remarkable resilience despite repeated efforts to stamp it out not only by the Ugandan and Congolese governments, but also the United Nations peacekeeping forced deployed in the Congo. The movement's leader, Jamil Mukulu, was trained in Afghanistan and Pakistan, where he associated with al-Qaeda, before returning to East Africa to launch the ADF with support from a number of foreign jihadist groups and the witting or unwitting help of several Islamic charities. The key to the group's survival has been its successful embedding in local and regional economic and commercial networks. Recently, there have been worrisome indicators that the group is becoming more active, killing more than several hundred people in recent months, including 5 who were beheaded in North Kivu just 2 weeks ago. And it can hardly be a coincidence that this very area is where East Africa's largest new discoveries of hydrocarbon reserves are located with production expected to begin in 2017, with much destined for domestic consumption. Time alone will tell whether the ADF evolves into the sort of threat that Boko Haram or al-Shabaab have posed or whether it degenerates into something more like the Lord's Resistance Army (LRA), a designated foreign terrorist group which, while brutish, does not actually represent the strategic threat to the United States and its allies posed by others so listed.

THE U.S. RESPONSE

This broad survey permits the drawing of several conclusions about the U.S. response to terrorism in Africa and the possible threats posed to U.S. persons and interests abroad as well as the American homeland.

First, time and again, the mistake has been made to underestimate—if not to discount entirely—the threat faced. Part of this is attributable to an analytical bias to limit future possibilities to extrapolations from the past, a hermeneutical choice which ignores the dynamic potential which many terrorist organizations have exhibited. Another part of the explanation is even more basic: The sheer lack of resources for Africa-related intelligence and analysis across the whole of the U.S. Government. Given the geopolitical, economic, and security stakes, the failure to invest more in institutions, personnel, training, and strategic focus is incredibly shortsighted.

Second, with the exception of the Department of Defense with the U.S. Africa Command (USAFRICOM), across the U.S. Government there is an artificial division of the continent that, quite frankly, is rejected not only by Africans, but is also unhelpful. If one looks, for example, at the North African states which are usually grouped with the Middle East, there are few compelling geopolitical, economic, or strategic reasons to do so except for Egypt. In point of fact, the overwhelming majority of the regional political, security, and commercial links extending to and from the other four countries of the Maghreb go north-south across the Sahara, not east-west towards the Levant. While ad hoc arrangements such as the State Department's designation of Ambassador Dan Mozena to coordinate diplomatic efforts across the Sahel are helpful, longer-term solutions would be preferable.

Third, USAFRICOM, the geographic command responsible for implementing whatever military operations, including counterterrorism operations, are eventually deemed necessary on the African continent, whether by assisting African partners or taking direct action, has since its establishment been hampered by less than adequate resources—and this was before sequestration kicked in and fiscal austerity became *de rigueur*—to carry out its ordinary assigned mission, to say nothing of extraordinary challenges which have arisen in recent years within its area of responsibility. While the three successive commanders of USAFRICOM have managed as well as they could, often adroitly juggling resources and priorities, clearly a more sustainable approach is required.

Fourth, closely related to terrorism is the danger posed by lack of effective sovereignty that bedevils many African governments. Often the challenge first manifests itself in criminality, whether in the form of piracy and other brigandage or in that of trafficking, human or material. While the Somali piracy threat—which, at its height, had several linkages to the extremists of al-Shabaab—has been generally diminished, attacks on commercial shipping have been on the uptick in the Gulf of Guinea. Moreover, West Africa has seen an explosion in drug trafficking, both as transshipments towards Europe and other destinations and, even more worrisome, for local consumption. Similarly, in the ever-creative pursuit of funding for their violence, both insurgents and terrorists have also turned to poaching. Studies have exhaustively documented how armed groups ranging from rebels in Mozambique to al-Shabaab in Somalia to fugitive Ugandan warlord Joseph Kony and the remaining fighters in his Lord's Resistance Army (LRA) to Séléka militiamen in the Central African Republic, among all-too-many others, have systematically exploited weak governance and porous borders to carry out their grisly trade, increasingly in partnership with organized criminal networks. For the United States, all this means that increasing vigilance against terrorism in Africa also requires greater investments in law enforcement capabilities focused on the continent, including enhanced analytical resources at home, more liaison personnel posted abroad, and stepping up efforts to build the capacity of our partners on the continent.

Fifth, as America's relationships—diplomatic, security, economic, and cultural—with Africa as a whole and the individual countries on the continent expands and deepens—a positive development to be sure—an unfortunate downside is that the potential risk to U.S. persons and interests as well as to the homeland necessarily increases. Quite simply, the threats are there and, by its very nature, more engagement also increases exposure and vulnerability. The answer is not to curtail engagement since there are clear strategic imperatives for seeking to build these links, but to ensure that adequate resources are mustered to cope with the meet the rising demand across a whole range of sectors from civil aviation to ports to customs and immigration, etc., for intelligence about and security against threats originating in Africa.

Sixth, the challenge of terrorism in Africa and any derivative threat to the United States cannot be addressed except in an integrated fashion, with solutions that embrace a broader notion of human security writ large—encompassing social, economic, and political development—which, often enough, also must transcend national and other artificial boundaries. This obviously is not a task for the United States alone, but is one which it is in America's strategic interest to embrace and to lead.

CONCLUSION

The administration's *2012 U.S. Strategy Toward Sub-Saharan Africa* rightly characterized Africa as "more important than ever to the security and prosperity of the international community, and to the United States in particular." The administration and the Congress deserve credit for efforts over the last few years to shift the narrative on Africa towards a greater focus on the extraordinary opportunities on the continent. However, if this momentum is to be maintained and those opportunities grasped, the United States needs to redouble its own efforts and also work closely with its African partners to manage the challenges and overcome terrorism and other the threats to security which stand in the way to an incredibly promising future.

Mr. KING. Doctor, thank you very much.

Again, usually we give more extensive introductions, but in view of the time factor we would rather hear from what you have to say rather than my introductions.

But with that, I am pleased to welcome back Tom Joscelyn, to the committee and subcommittee. He has testified here a number of times.

He is a senior fellow at the Foundation for Defense of Democracies and senior editor of *The Long War Journal,* a widely-read publication dealing with counterterrorism and related issues. Much of Mr. Joscelyn's research focuses on how al-Qaeda and its affiliates operate around the globe, and he is also a frequent contributor to the *Weekly Standard.* I have to say that often I take advice from him without giving him proper credit.

So I plagiarize quite a bit off you, Tom.

With that, recognize the gentleman.

STATEMENT OF THOMAS JOSCELYN, SENIOR FELLOW, FOUNDATION FOR DEFENSE OF DEMOCRACIES

Mr. JOSCELYN. Now, thank you, Chairman King. I guess that is what I am here for, actually, is to get plagiarized, so that is good.

But thank you, Chairman King, Ranking Member Higgins, other Members of the committee, and Ms. Wilson, for sitting here today and listening to this conversation—leading this conversation on the threats emerging from Africa. Like my colleague, Dr. Pham, here, I believe that oftentimes this committee is on the leading edge and sort-of ahead of the curve in terms of understanding evolving threats to American National security, and I think the situation in Africa today certainly does not bode well for the future.

Unfortunately, jihadism is a growth industry in Africa, and that is whether you are talking about the Islamic State, or ISIS, as it is often referred to, or al-Qaeda. Both sides of this rivalry have been growing at a very fast rate, I would say, in Africa overall over the last several years.

The primary victims of their terrorism are, in fact, of course, Africans and locals across the African continent. That doesn't mean that that there is no threat to the United States or our interests, or potentially the U.S. homeland. In fact, we have seen that threats to local populations abroad are oftentimes leading indicators of threats to us.

And, for example, Ranking Member Higgins mentioned the 1998 U.S. embassy bombings. The primary victims of those bombings in Kenya and Tanzania were, in fact, local Africans; they weren't— they didn't actually kill a lot of Americans in those attacks. But it was clearly a leading indicator of things to come when it came to threats to the U.S. National security both here at home and abroad.

So looking at it in that comprehensive sort of integrated manner, I applaud you, Chairman King. I know you constantly look at it that way, that it is one sort of holistic picture of what is going on in the world. I think that is the right way to look at it.

And in particular, with both ISIS and al-Qaeda in Africa, it is true that most of their victims are going to be local Africans, Muslims, people along those lines. That is a strategic liability for them because in their messaging, the more we can amplify the fact that they are killing Muslims and killing people locally in Africa, the bigger win that is for us because it rolls back their attempts to sort-of recruit and indoctrinate further people to their cause.

That is something we have to constantly be mindful of, that we actually have many, many allies across the African continent that we need to work with more closely in terms of messaging, and strategy, and those types of things.

But both ISIS and al-Qaeda have strategies for growth in Africa. The ISIS strategy is pretty clear-cut. We can all see it. You know, they are beheading people openly in Libya; they produce these gruesome, gory propaganda videos.

The Islamic State wants you to believe they are basically everywhere at all times. They want to announce their presence; they want to give you this sense that they are this ever-expanding caliphate.

ISIS clearly has grown rapidly in Africa. There is no doubt about that. My arguments aren't meant to diminish that growth or characterize that growth as anything but threatening to us.

However, I find that oftentimes the reporting sort-of misses the bigger picture, because al-Qaeda's strategy for Africa is exactly the opposite. Al-Qaeda's strategy for Africa is they don't want you to think they are anywhere. They want you to believe they are almost nowhere.

So what al-Qaeda has been doing inside Africa is they have today—and just off the top of my head here I counted about 10 different organizations which are clandestine al-Qaeda fronts across Africa, which are still openly loyal to al-Qaeda's leadership. What they are doing is they are trying to inculcate their ideology in these local causes across Africa.

This is something that is very nefarious and something that, as we expose them and show that they are, in fact, not part of the local population and that they don't actually represent local interests, that can help turn back their strategy.

Finally, I will say something about the threats to the United States and how these can concretely be manifested over time.

I brought with me here today as a prop some of the declassified documents from bin Laden's compound. In fact, all the declassified documents that we have got available to us publicly from bin Laden's compound are in this folder right here.

What is interesting is that bin Laden clearly saw Africa and the African branches of al-Qaeda as part of a comprehensive strategy. In fact, he integrated what they were doing in Africa into al-Qaeda's global designs. Those designs include, of course, threats to the U.S. homeland.

Some of the things you can see in these documents are, for example, that the leaders of al-Qaeda's branches in Africa were, on more than one occasion, turned into the heads of al-Qaeda's operations against us. So in other words, they took guys who were leading al-

Qaeda in the Islamic Maghreb, leading the fight in Shabaab, and they became external operations chiefs for al-Qaeda globally. That is, these are guys who then would—actually were tasked with figuring out ways to come after us.

Second, you can also see that Osama bin Laden, as you mentioned, Congressman, actually ordered his branches in Africa to designate or find candidates who were suitable for attacks right here in the United States. So he put the order out to al-Qaeda's African branches and said, ''Find guys who can actually go to the United States and commit attacks, and they are going to be referred up the chain of command and we are going to use them.''

Finally, what Osama bin Laden said was that the branches of al-Qaeda in Africa have to integrate their work with the other parts of al-Qaeda, including the external operations capability. So, as I say in my written testimony and go into this at some length, al-Qaeda is structured with regional branches where they have emirs, or leaders, who are in charge of their regional areas. They have two official regional branches in Africa—al-Qaeda in the Islamic Maghreb and Shabaab.

But bin Laden specifically ordered these branches to coordinate their work with the external operations part of al-Qaeda, which is tasked with coming after us. So in other words, this is a much more cohesive challenge, I would say, when you actually get into what they say themselves about how they operate and their functioning than I think the public discourse oftentimes lets on.

I will leave it at there.

[The prepared statement of Mr. Joscelyn follows:]

PREPARED STATEMENT OF THOMAS JOSCELYN

APRIL 29, 2015

Chairman King, Ranking Member Higgins, and Members of the committee, thank you for inviting me here today to discuss the threat posed by jihadist groups in Africa. In Chairman King's announcement of this hearing, he rightly argued that while much attention has been given to the threats posed by the Islamic State of Iraq and Syria (ISIS) and al-Qaeda in the heart of the Middle East and South Asia, ''we must also focus on the imminent and growing threat posed by their affiliates operating in Africa.''[1] Indeed, the jihadist organizations headquartered outside of Africa are strongly tied to various groups operating inside the continent. Both ISIS (or the Islamic State) and al-Qaeda maintain international networks that stretch across Africa.

In preparing today's testimony, I reviewed the history of al-Qaeda's plotting against the West. A number of facts demonstrate that al-Qaeda's presence in Africa has been tied to these efforts. For instance, declassified documents recovered in Osama bin Laden's compound show that he ordered al-Qaeda's branches in Africa to select candidates capable of striking inside the United States. Bin Laden also ordered al-Qaeda's African branches to coordinate their work with his ''external operations'' team, which was responsible for plotting attacks against Western interests. Some of al-Qaeda's most senior leaders, including those who have overseen al-Qaeda's planned attacks in the West, have come from Africa. Senior al-Qaeda leaders embedded in Shabaab have also trained operatives to attack in Europe. I discuss this evidence in detail in the final section of my written testimony.

Complex tribal, ethnic, and religious dynamics mean that any summary of the situation in Africa will be necessarily incomplete. However, I will attempt to distill some themes that are important for understanding the rising jihadist threat in the continent. While there are important differences between ISIS and al-Qaeda, and the two are at odds with one another in a variety of ways, they are both inherently

---

[1] *http://homeland.house.gov/hearing/subcommittee-hearing-terrorism-africa-imminent-threat-united-states.*

anti-American and anti-Western. Thus, they constitute a threat to our interests everywhere their jihadists fight.

Since the beginning of the year, the ISIS branch in Libya has repeatedly attacked foreign interests. The group has bombed and/or assaulted with small arms the Algerian, Moroccan, Iranian, South Korean, and Spanish embassies in Tripoli. Fortunately, these attacks have caused only a few casualties, as foreign governments pulled most of their diplomatic personnel out of Libya months ago. But these incidents show the organization's followers are deeply hostile to any foreign presence.

Other ISIS attacks on foreigners in Libya have been more lethal and at least two Americans have been killed by ISIS's so-called "provinces." In January, the group's fighters launched a complex assault on the Corinthia Hotel in Tripoli. Ten people, including David Berry, a former U.S. Marine serving as a security contractor, were killed.[2] In August 2014, jihadists from the ISIS province in the Sinai killed William Henderson, an American petroleum worker.[3]

Some of ISIS's most gruesome acts in North Africa have come with pointed threats against the West. In February, the jihadists beheaded 21 Egyptian Copts. The propaganda video showing the murders was entitled, "A Message Signed with Blood to the Nation of the Cross." ISIS explicitly threatened Italy in the video and also made it clear that they would target Christians simply for adhering to a different faith. Earlier this month, ISIS's branch followed up by killing a large group of Ethiopian Christians.

In March, ISIS claimed responsibility for the massacre at the Bardo National Museum in Tunis. More than 20 people were killed in the assault, which targeted foreign tourists. Citizens of Britain, France, Colombia, Germany, Italy, Japan, Poland, and Spain were among the victims. Although ISIS was quick to lay claim to the museum slayings, the reality is more complicated.[4] The Tunisian government has blamed the Uqba ibn Nafi Brigade, which is part of al-Qaeda in the Islamic Maghreb (AQIM), an official branch of al-Qaeda.[5] Based on publicly-available information, it appears that the attackers may have joined ISIS, but the operation itself was planned by the AQIM brigade's leadership.

Al-Qaeda's international network continues to launch high-profile attacks across the continent. Some of these operations directly target foreigners. Earlier this month, Shabaab, al-Qaeda's official branch in Somalia, killed more than 140 people at the Garissa University College in Kenya. The gunmen reportedly separated out non-Muslims for killing, letting many Muslims go.[6] This shows that the organization, like other parts of al-Qaeda, is very concerned about the impact of its violence in the Muslim-majority world. In this respect and others, the Garissa attack was similar to Shabaab's siege of the Westgate shopping mall in September 2013. More than 60 people were killed, with Shabaab's gunmen singling out non-Muslims. Shabaab's attacks in Kenya and other neighboring countries are part of what the United Nations has identified as the group's "regional" strategy.[7] Shabaab has undoubtedly suffered setbacks since the height of its power in East Africa, but it still operates a prolific insurgency inside Somalia, while also seeking to expand its capabilities in the surrounding countries. In fact, America's counterterrorism efforts in East Africa seem to be principally aimed at the part of Shabaab tasked with exporting terrorism throughout the region.[8]

As we've seen over the past several years, al-Qaeda-affiliated groups in Africa will attack American and Western interests when the opportunity presents itself. The September 11, 2012 attack on the U.S. Mission and Annex in Benghazi and the raid

[2] Rich Schapiro, "Gunmen take hostages in luxury Libyan hotel, kill 8 including 1 American," *New York Daily News*, January 27, 2015; (*http://www.nydailynews.com/news/world/gunmen-hostages-libyan-hotel-kill-3-guards-article-1.2093208*).

[3] Cassandra Vinograd, Charlene Gubash, and Gabe Gutierrez, "ISIS-Linked Ansar Beit al-Maqdis Says It Killed U.S. Oil Worker William Henderson," nbcnews.com, December 1, 2014; (*http://www.nbcnews.com/storyline/isis-terror/isis-linked-ansar-beit-al-maqdis-says-it-killed-u-n258786*).

[4] Daveed Gartenstein-Ross, "Did the Islamic State Exaggerate Its Role in the Bardo Museum Attack?", FDD Policy Brief, March 30, 2015; (*http://www.defenddemocracy.org/media-hit/gartenstein-ross-daveed-did-the-islamic-state-exaggerate-its-role-in-the-bardo-museum-attack/*).

[5] Yaqin Hussam al-Din, "Algeria and Tunisia join forces to fight 'terrorism'," *al-Araby-al-Jadeed*, March 30, 2015; (*http://www.alaraby.co.uk/english/politics/2015/4/1/algeria-and-tunisia-join-forces-to-fight-terrorism*).

[6] "Somali Islamist rebels claim attack on Kenyan university: spokesman," *Reuters*, April 2, 2015.

[7] United Nations Security Council, "Report of the Monitoring Group on Somalia and Eritrea pursuant to Security Council resolution 2060 (2012)," July 12, 2013.

[8] Bill Roggio, "US targets senior Shabaab intelligence official in airstrike," *The Long War Journal*, March 14, 2015; (*http://www.longwarjournal.org/archives/2015/03/us-targets-senior-shabaab-intelligence-official-in-airstrike.php*).

on the U.S. Embassy in Tunis 3 days later were carried out by al-Qaeda-linked groups.[9] The Ansar al Sharia organizations in Libya and Tunisia, both of which are tied to AQIM, were involved in these assaults on America's diplomatic presence in North Africa. In early 2013, terrorists commanded by Mokhtar Belmokhtar killed dozens of foreign workers during the siege of the In Amenas gas facility in Algeria. Belmokhtar, who is openly loyal to Ayman al Zawahiri, claimed responsibility for operation on behalf of al-Qaeda.

There is no doubt, therefore, that both ISIS and al-Qaeda pose a threat to Western interests in Africa. Below, I explore current trends within both organizations, highlighting some ways these international networks may threaten Americans both home and abroad. But first, I briefly look at the different strategies ISIS and al-Qaeda are employing to build up their networks.

TWO RIVAL JIHADIST MODELS

In Africa, as elsewhere, we are witnessing two rival models vying for power among jihadists. While ISIS and al-Qaeda share some of the same long-term goals, the two sides have adopted radically different approaches to marketing their ideology and expanding their base of support.

ISIS uses consistent branding, describing its followers around the world as part of a growing ''caliphate'' led by Abu Bakr al Baghdadi (the self-proclaimed caliph ''Ibrahim I''). ISIS branches are branded as the caliphate's ''provinces,'' whether they control significant territory or not. ISIS also markets its over-the-top brutality to project strength and intimidate its enemies. (Al-Qaeda long ago decided that ISIS's tactics, such as beheadings, were counterproductive for its cause.) The organization wants both its supporters and its foes to believe it is an ever-expanding menace that cannot be stopped. Because the group is so heavily invested in this type of messaging, it is relatively easy to track the organization's international organization. Of course, certain aspects of ISIS's operations remain hidden from public view. But ISIS broadcasts its presence around the world as loudly as it can.

Al-Qaeda, on the other hand, has adopted precisely the opposite approach. Whereas ISIS wants people to see its international footprint, al-Qaeda goes to great lengths to hide much, but not all, of its organizational structure. Al-Qaeda's strategy is far more clandestine in nature. In contrast to ISIS's uniform branding, al-Qaeda has adopted numerous brands, which serve to mask the extent of its influence, inculcate al-Qaeda's radical ideology in local populations, and attract support from individuals, organizations and governments that may not want to be seen as openly assisting al-Qaeda. All of this makes tracking al-Qaeda's international network a far more difficult task.

Al-Qaeda has played this game—using multiple brands, masking the extent of its influence—repeatedly in Africa. Consider the following examples. In February 2012, Shabaab in Somalia and al-Qaeda's senior leadership announced their formal merger.[10] Some analysts have incorrectly argued that Osama bin Laden rejected a formal merger when he was alive, and it was his successor, Ayman al-Zawahiri, who decided to merge with Shabaab. But documents recovered in Osama bin Laden's compound tell a different story. Bin Laden thought of Shabaab as part of al-Qaeda's international network well before his death.[11] Bin Laden devoted al-Qaeda's resources to helping Shabaab. For example, he assigned one of his key lieutenants to research Shabaab's governance efforts and the applicable sharia laws. The al-Qaeda master simply didn't want to announce the relationship, because he feared it would bring more international pressure on the East African group and limit its ability

[9] The U.S. Senate Select Committee on Intelligence and other official entities have confirmed the role of multiple al-Qaeda-affiliated groups in the Benghazi attack. See, for example: Thomas Joscelyn, ''Senate report: Terrorists 'affiliated' with multiple al-Qaeda groups involved in Benghazi attack,'' *The Long War Journal*, January 15, 2014; (*http://www.longwarjournal.org/archives/2014/01/intelligence\on\al.php*).

[10] Bill Roggio and Thomas Joscelyn, ''Shabaab formally joins al-Qaeda,'' *The Long War Journal*, February 9, 2012; (*http://www.longwarjournal.org/archives/2012/02/shabaab\for-mally\joi.php*).

[11] See Government Exhibit 425 in the trial of Abid Naseer. The document, dated August 7, 2010, is a letter written from Osama bin Laden to Atiyah Abd al Rahman. It can be found here: *http://www.scribd.com/doc/257160502/Bin-Laden-raid-documents*.

to raise funds from wealthy donors throughout the Gulf.[12] In other words, bin Laden sought to conceal al-Qaeda's relationship with Shabaab as much as possible.[13]

Similarly, AQIM does not typically advertise its links to the aforementioned Ansar al Sharia groups in Libya and Tunisia. However, both the United Nations' National Security Council and the U.S. Government have formally recognized those connections.[14] Indeed, Ansar al Sharia Libya was led by an al-Qaeda loyalist named Mohammed al Zahawi. But Zahawi's past, including the fact that he had personally met with Osama bin Laden in the 1990s and adopted al-Qaeda's jihadist program, did not become publicly known until after Zahawi's death was confirmed.[15] Astute observers could see from the beginning that these Ansar al Sharia groups were operating as part of al-Qaeda's international network, but al-Qaeda does not advertise this relationship the same way ISIS markets its presence in North Africa. This has led to much confusion in the public reporting.

In a report published in August 2012 (''Al Qaeda in Libya: A Profile''), the Defense Department's Combating Terrorism Technical Support Office (CTTSO) concluded that al-Qaeda had a clandestine strategy for building up its presence inside Libya.[16] The CTTSO surmised that al-Qaeda was using alternative names, such as Ansar al Sharia, to hide its designs and that senior terrorists inside the country were communicating with al-Qaeda's senior leadership in Pakistan. Documents recovered in Osama bin Laden's compound show that al-Qaeda operatives were, in fact, dispatched to Libya early on in the uprisings against Muammar al Qaddafi.[17] They were tasked with organizing al-Qaeda's efforts, but their presence was unannounced.

These are just some examples of how al-Qaeda deliberately hides its presence in African countries.[18] This simple tactic has led to some deep biases in the public reporting on jihadism in Africa and elsewhere. Namely, the extent of al-Qaeda's international network is consistently *underestimated*. And, in some ways, ISIS's international presence has been *overestimated*. For instance, when fighters loyal to ISIS held a parade in Derna last year, multiple press outlets reported that ISIS had taken full control of the Libyan city. Some reports make this claim to this day, even though it is obvious that other jihadist groups still have a significant presence in Derna and ISIS does not dominate the city in its entirety.

This observation is not intended to downplay the seriousness of ISIS's international expansion. ISIS's ''provinces'' have grown dramatically in some key areas. But exposing al-Qaeda's clandestine strategy provides key context for understanding the unfolding story inside Africa.

OVERVIEW OF THE ISIS PRESENCE IN AFRICA

In this section, I provide a sketch of the ISIS presence in Africa. It is important to note that while ISIS has grown in Africa, numerous reports and analyses have

---

[12] SOCOM–2012–0000005. The document, dated August 7, 2010, is a letter from bin Laden to Mukhtar Abu al Zubayr, who was the emir of Shabaab at the time. This document was released in 2012. Bin Laden sets forth his reasons for not announcing the relationship in this letter. It is an attachment to Government Exhibit 425, which is referenced above and was released earlier this year. Bin Laden also explains his reasoning in Exhibit 425.

[13] Bin Laden's two letters explaining why Shabaab should hide its relationship with al-Qaeda are dated August 7, 2010. Incredibly, my colleague Bill Roggio reported just over 1 week later, on August 15, 2010, that bin Laden told Shabaab to keep the relationship secret. See: Bill Roggio, ''Al Qaeda advises Shabaab to keep low profile on links, attack US interests,'' *The Long War Journal*, August 15, 2010; (*http://www.longwarjournal.org/archives/2010/08/allqaedaladviseslsha.php*).

[14] See, for example: Thomas Joscelyn, ''UN recognizes ties between Ansar al Sharia in Libya, al-Qaeda,'' *The Long War Journal*, November 19, 2014; (*http://www.longwarjournal.org/archives/2014/11/unldesignateslansar.php*).

[15] Thomas Joscelyn, ''Ansar al Sharia Libya leader met with Osama bin Laden, followed his 'methodology','' *The Long War Journal*, February 11, 2015; (*http://www.longwarjournal.org/archives/2015/02/ansarlallsharialliby12.php*).

[16] The report can be found here: *http://fas.org/irp/world/para/aq-libya-loc.pdf*. For a summary of the report, see: Thomas Joscelyn, ''Al Qaeda's plan for Libya highlighted in congressional report,'' *The Long War Journal*, September 21, 2012; (*http://www.longwarjournal.org/archives/2012/09/allqaedaslplanlforll.php*).

[17] See Government Exhibit 431 in the trial of Abid Naseer. This letter to bin Laden was written by Atiyah Abd al Rahman in early April 2011. For more on this issue, see: Thomas Joscelyn, ''Osama Bin Laden's Files: The Arab revolutions,'' *The Long War Journal*, March 3, 2015; (*http://www.longwarjournal.org/archives/2015/03/osama-bin-ladens-files-the-arab-revolutions.php*).

[18] Al-Qaeda has employed the same practice elsewhere. In Syria, for example, al-Qaeda's leaders tried to hide their relationship with the al-Nusrah Front, a regional branch of the organization. Some of the other ''rebel'' groups in Syria are clearly unannounced al-Qaeda front organizations.

inaccurately characterized the manner in which the organization has grown. For example, some claimed that AQIM was going to defect to ISIS. There is no evidence that this was considered a serious possibility by AQIM's senior leadership. The organization has explicitly rejected ISIS's claim to rule as a caliphate, reaffirming its allegiance to Ayman al-Zawahiri in the process. Similarly, speculative reports have claimed that Shabaab may defect to ISIS. While it is certainly possible that factions within Shabaab may want to join ISIS, there is no indication that the overall organization plans to do so. In fact, Shabaab's propaganda over the past several months has continued to advertise its role in al-Qaeda's network.

Still, the ISIS presence in Africa is worrisome for many reasons. As explained above, ISIS's branches have repeatedly attacked foreign interests, while also threatening the West. Consider the following additional observations:

- *The ISIS presence in Africa has grown significantly over the past year, especially in Libya, Tunisia, and the Sinai.*—The ISIS announced its merger with a wing of Ansar Bayt al Maqdis ("ABM") late last year, turning the group into one of its so-called "provinces."[19] ISIS's growth in Libya and Tunisia has been fueled mainly by young jihadists. Fighters returning to their home countries from Iraq and Syria have provided a pool of resources for ISIS. As of this writing, ISIS has a major presence in the city of Sirte and significant contingents in Benghazi and Derna, as well as elsewhere in Libya. While Ansar al Sharia in Libya and Tunisia have not defected to ISIS, the "caliphate" has successfully poached some members and leaders from these groups. For example, Ansar al Sharia Libya's chief sharia official in Benghazi joined ISIS earlier this year.
- *ISIS gained a significant footing in West Africa by merging with Boko Haram earlier this year.*—The first indications of the ISIS-Boko Haram relationship could be seen in the latter's propaganda, which has been typically poor. Over the past several months, Boko Haram's propaganda became significantly better, showing multiple signs of ISIS's influence. ISIS likely sent a team to Nigeria to improve Boko Haram's media capabilities and to negotiate the alliance. Boko Haram now calls itself the Islamic State in West Africa, or the Islamic State's Province in West Africa.
- *In Algeria, a small group of AQIM commanders has defected to ISIS.*—Prior to their defection, virtually no one had even heard of them. However, ISIS's Algerian arm has already committed some attacks, including the beheading of a French hostage last year.[20]
- *ISIS's "provinces" in Africa are part of an international network, so their operations are not confined to the continent.*—For instance, Libya and Tunisia have probably contributed more jihadists, on a per capita basis, to the jihad in Iraq and Syria than any other countries. This facilitation pipeline has existed since the height of the Iraq War. ISIS has used this recruiting network to build its presence in North Africa by sending some key leaders and fighting units back to their home countries. Saudis, Yemenis, and other nationalities have also been identified as being among ISIS's main leaders in Libya.
- *ISIS's expansion in Africa is not just aimed at growing support from local recruits, but is also part of its on-going effort to attract foreign fighters from around the world.*—Through mid-2014, the Islamic State was focused on recruiting foreigners for its battles in Iraq and Syria. Since then, the group has increasingly called for foreign fighters to join its cause in African hotspots. When announcing its merger with Boko Haram, for example, the Islamic State's spokesman specifically called on new recruits to join the "caliphate" in West Africa if they could not make the trip to the heart of the Middle East or elsewhere. "All Muslims, you should all come to your State, for we are calling on you to mobilize for jihad," ISIS spokesman Abu Muhammad al Adnani said in March. He continued: "We incite you and call upon you to immigrate for jihad and to immigrate to your brothers in West Africa."[21] Just in the past few days, a Libyan ISIS fighter released a message calling on recruits to join him in North Africa. Similarly, there have been some limited efforts to turn the Sinai into a destination for foreign fighters.[22]

---

[19] Another Egyptian group, Ajnad Misr, broke off from ABM and appears to be an al-Qaeda front group. Ajnad Misr has not joined ISIS.

[20] Ishaan Tharoor, "Islamic State-linked group beheads French national in Algeria," *The Washington Post*, September 24, 2014; (*http://www.washingtonpost.com/blogs/worldviews/wp/2014/09/24/islamic-state-linked-group-beheads-french-national-in-algeria/*).

[21] SITE Intelligence Group, "IS Spokesman Threatens Enemy to Convert or Be Subjugated, Accepts Boko Haram's Pledge of Allegiance," March 12, 2015.

[22] Thomas Joscelyn, "Islamic State supporters advertise Sinai as jihadist destination," *The Long War Journal*, December 1, 2014; (*http://www.longwarjournal.org/archives/2014/12/islamic\state\suppor.php*).

- *There is evidence that at least one potential American recruit saw Libya as a viable destination for waging jihad on behalf of ISIS.*—The FBI has alleged that Specialist Hasan R. Edmonds, a member of the Army National Guard in Illinois, intended "to travel overseas and fight on behalf of" ISIS. The investigation allegedly revealed that Edmonds was willing to join ISIS in North Africa. "I am fine being in Egypt, Sham, or Libya to be honest akhi [brother]," the defendant said in one conversation, according to the FBI. "I just want to answer the call."[23] Edmonds reportedly wanted to join ISIS's ranks in Derna, Libya.[24] Authorities have also charged Jonas Edmonds, Hasan's cousin, with "planning an attack at a military base in Northern Illinois where Specialist Edmonds had been training."[25] Of course, other Americans have been drawn to ISIS in Iraq and Syria.[26] There is a possibility that more of them will seek out jihad in Africa instead.
- *A notorious terrorist who helped recruit the 9/11 suicide pilots has reportedly helped ISIS grow its footprint in Egypt.*—According to a credible report, Mohammed Zammar, who helped recruit al-Qaeda's Hamburg cell for the 9/11 plot, has joined ISIS. Zammar had been imprisoned by the Assad regime in Syria, but was freed as part of a prisoner exchange with ISIS. In return for securing his freedom, Zammar joined ISIS and reportedly helped the organization woo Ansar Bayt al Maqdis in the Sinai to its cause. Zammar even traveled to the Sinai to close the deal.[27] This is troubling because it means that a jihadist who is adept at recruiting Westernized jihadists is traveling freely. It is possible that Zammar could once again help recruit young jihadists for a special operation in the West.

OVERVIEW OF AL-QAEDA'S PRESENCE IN AFRICA

While ISIS gets most of the headlines these days, al-Qaeda is still a major player in Africa. In this section, I rely heavily on declassified documents captured in Osama bin Laden's compound to explain how al-Qaeda is structured in Africa.[28] The bin Laden files demonstrate that al-Qaeda has a much more cohesive international infrastructure than is commonly believed. While that infrastructure has undoubtedly evolved, especially with the loss of some leaders, it is unwise to assume that it has been eliminated entirely. Indeed, there are multiple indications that the al-Qaeda bureaucracy established under bin Laden lives on. The following points will hopefully illuminate the threat posed by al-Qaeda's network inside the continent:

- *Al-Qaeda has two official, regional branches in Africa: Al-Qaeda in the Islamic Maghreb (AQIM) and Shabaab in Somalia.*—The leaders of both organizations have sworn *bayat* (oath of allegiance) to al-Qaeda's senior leadership. The leaders of both organizations remain openly loyal to Ayman al Zawahiri, al-Qaeda's emir. While AQIM and Shabaab are often called al-Qaeda "affiliates," al-Qaeda refers to them as "regions" or "branches." Osama bin Laden also used the phrase "regional areas" to describe al-Qaeda's presence in various places.[29] This terminology helps to better understand how al-Qaeda is actually organized. Each regional emir oversees al-Qaeda's efforts in his designated area. So, AQIM emir Abu Musab Abdel Wadoud (a.k.a. Abdelmalek Droukdel) is in charge of al-Qaeda's efforts in North Africa, west of Egypt, stretching down into Mali.

[23] See Affidavit of FBI Special Agent Morgan A. Spurlock, March 25, 2015. The affidavit can be accessed online at: *http://www.washingtonpost.com/r/2010-2019/WashingtonPost/2015/03/26/National-Security/Graphics/Edmonds%20Complaint.pdf.*

[24] Michael S. Schmidt, "National Guardsman Accused of Trying to Join ISIS in Libya," *The New York Times*, March 26, 2015; (*http://www.nytimes.com/2015/03/27/us/guardsman-accused-of-trying-to-join-isis-in-libya.html*).

[25] Ibid.

[26] Just days ago, authorities charged six Somali-Americans with seeking to join ISIS. See Scott Shane, "6 Minnesotans Held in Plot to Join ISIS," *The New York Times*, April 20, 2015; (*http://www.nytimes.com/2015/04/21/us/6-somali-americans-arrested-in-isis-recruiting-case.html*).

[27] Bruce Riedel, "Baghdadi vs. Zawahri: Battle for Global Jihad," *Al-Monitor*, December 1, 2014; (*http://www.usnews.eom/news/articles/2014/12/01/baghdadi-vs-zawahri-battle-for-global-jihad*).

[28] All of the bin Laden files referenced in this section can be found on two websites: *https://www.ctc.usma.edu/posts/letters-from-abbottabad-bin-ladin-sidelined* and *http://www.scribd.com/doc/257160502/Bin-Laden-raid-documents.*

[29] SOCOM–2012–0000019. This is a letter written by Osama bin Laden in May 2010 and addressed to Atiyah Abd al Rahman. Bin Laden wrote, "We are now in a new phase of assessing Jihad activities and developing them beyond what they were in the past two areas, military activity and media releases. Our work in these two areas is broad and sweeping, encompassing the headquarters and regional areas."

Shabaab's emir, Ahmed Diriye (a.k.a. Sheikh Ahmad Umar and Abu Ubaidah), is generally in charge of al-Qaeda's efforts in Somalia and East Africa.

• *Al-Qaeda designates certain operatives to work on what it calls "external operations," or "external work," which includes spectacular terrorist attacks against Western interests.*—Osama bin Laden ordered al-Qaeda's regional emirs, including the head of AQIM, to coordinate their efforts with the deputies he put in charge of al-Qaeda's "external work." The al-Qaeda deputy in charge of "external operations" from 2010 until his capture in September 2011 was Yunis al Mauritani. Al Mauritani was recently sentenced to a lengthy prison in his home country. Bin Laden set forth a specific chain of command to oversee "external operations." Yunis al Mauritani reported to Atiyah Abd al Rahman (then al-Qaeda's general manager), who answered to bin Laden himself.

In his letters to Rahman, bin Laden stressed that each of al-Qaeda's "regions" must coordinate all "external work" with his deputies. He even wanted Rahman to inform "the brothers in Yemen" (AQAP) "that working in the sea, even within the territorial waters of the [Arabian] Peninsula, is to be considered external work that requires coordination with you."[30] In another declassified document, bin Laden made it clear that al Mauritani was "in-charge of the external operations in Africa, except the Islamic Maghreb states, starting from Libya to Mauritania, which is under the control of brother Abu Musa'b 'Abd-al-Wadud [the emir of AQIM], and the African horn, which is under the control of the Emir of Al-Shabaab Mujahideen Movement."[31]

• *Osama bin Laden ordered each of al-Qaeda's branches, including AQIM in Africa, to identify recruits capable of launching attacks inside the United States.*— "It would be nice if you would ask the brothers in all regions if they have a brother distinguished by his good manners, integrity, courage, and secretiveness, who can operate in the U.S.," bin Laden wrote to his top manager, Atiyah Abd al Rahman, in May 2010.[32] Bin Laden explained that an operative selected to attack the United States should be able to "live there, or it should be easy for him to travel there."[33] And each regional emir "should tell us this without taking any action and also tell us whether or not [the chosen operative] is willing to conduct a suicide operation," bin Laden wrote.[34] Bin Laden continued: "It would be nice if you [Rahman] would send two messages—one to Brother Abu Mus'ab 'Abd-al-Wadud [the emir of AQIM], and the other to Brother Abu Basir Nasir al-Wuhayshi [the emir of AQAP]—and ask them to put forward their best in cooperating with Shaykh Yunis in whatever he asks of them."[35] Al-Qaeda's founder wanted AQIM to help pay for the operations: "Hint to the brothers in the Islamic Maghreb that they provide [Yunis al Mauritani] with the financial support that he might need in the next six months, to the tune of approximately 200,000 euros."[36]

• *Some of al-Qaeda's most senior leaders, including those tasked with overseeing external operations, have come from Africa.*—Saleh al Somali was al-Qaeda's external operations chief until his death in late 2009. Somali's jihadist pedigree stretched back to al-Qaeda's earliest efforts in eastern Africa, when the terror organization trained Somali militia to attack American forces. At the time of his death, Somali's close ties to Shabaab were considered especially problematic, given Shabaab's ability to recruit Americans.[37]

The aforementioned Yunis al Mauritani was al-Qaeda's external operations chief from 2010 until his capture in 2011. Al Mauritani "participated in the formation" of AQIM.[38] He joined the Salafist Group for Call and Combat (GSPC), AQIM's predecessor, in 2001 and was sent by GSPC's leadership to cement their

[30] SOCOM–2012–0000019, p. 33.

[31] Government Exhibit 427 in the trial of Abid Naseer. The letter is addressed to "Hajji Uthman," who is likely Saeed al Masri, al-Qaeda's general manager at the time. It was presumably authored by bin Laden. The context suggests it was written sometime after December 2009. The letter can be found here: *http://www.scribd.com/doc/257160502/Bin-Laden-raid-documents.*

[32] SOCOM–2012–0000019, p. 32.

[33] Ibid.

[34] Ibid.

[35] Ibid.

[36] Ibid.

[37] Bill Roggio, "Al Qaeda's external operations chief thought killed in US strike in Pakistan," *The Long War Journal*, December 11, 2009; (*http://www.longwarjournal.org/archives/2009/12/allqaedaslexternallo.php*).

[38] U.S. Treasury Department, "Treasury Targets Three Senior Al-Qa'ida Leaders," September 7, 2011; (*http://www.treasury.gov/press-center/press-releases/Pages/tgl289.aspx*).

deal with al-Qaeda in 200 7.[39] In 2010, he was in charge of a plan, backed by bin Laden, "to ostensibly damage the economy of Europe."[40]

The biographies of terrorists such as Somali and Mauritani show that al-Qaeda has used its presence in Africa to build a deep roster of talent.

- *Senior al-Qaeda operatives embedded within Shabaab's ranks have planned attacks in the West.*—As I testified before this committee in July 2011, senior al-Qaeda operatives have held some of Shabaab's most important positions since its earliest days.[41] And these operatives have been responsible for plotting attacks against Western and other foreign interests. One of these leaders, Fazul Abdullah Mohammed, was killed in 2011. Authorities found plans for attacking London in Fazul's possession.[42] A group known as the "London Boys" was trained by Fazul and reportedly tasked with executing attacks in the United Kingdom.[43]

- *AQAP's leaders are now al-Qaeda's general management team and they have worked closely with Shabaab, as well as with AQIM.*—Given that AQAP has led al-Qaeda's attempts to attack the U.S. homeland in recent years, it is possible that the group will seek to employ al-Qaeda's African assets against the West. In previous testimony, I highlighted the close ties between Shabaab and AQAP.[44] Since that time, AQAP's emir, Nasir al Wuhayshi, was named al-Qaeda's global general manager.[45] This role gives him broad power across all of al-Qaeda's branches. (Indeed, this is the same position that was held by Atiyah Abd al Rahman, who is discussed above.) Al-Qaeda documents first published by the Associated Press also show that Wuhayshi has been in close contact with the leadership of AQIM.[46]

  - *In addition to its two official branches, there are a number of other jihadist groups in Africa that are part of al-Qaeda's international network.*—The most significant organizations include: Ajnad Misr (Egypt), Ansar al Din (Mali), Ansar al Sharia Libya, Ansar al Sharia Tunisia (which has been inactive of late), Ansaru (Nigeria), Al Mourabitoun (North Africa and Mali) and the Uqba bin Nafi Brigade (Tunisia). Just recently, another new group called Al Muhajiroun (the "Emigrants of East Africa") was established. In its founding video, the group says it "owes allegiance" to the emir of Shabaab and Ayman al Zawahiri.

Mr. KING. Thank you, Mr. Joscelyn.

Our next witness, Dr. Daniel Byman, is director of research and a senior fellow in the Center for Middle East Policy at the Brookings Institution. His research focuses on counterterrorism and Middle East security. Dr. Byman is a professor in Georgetown University's security studies program, and he also served as a staff member on the 9/11 Commission and worked for the U.S. Government.

So, Dr. Byman, you are recognized. Thank you for being here.

STATEMENT OF DANIEL BYMAN, RESEARCH DIRECTOR, CENTER FOR MIDDLE EAST POLICY, CENTER FOR SECURITY STUDIES, BROOKINGS INSTITUTE

Mr. BYMAN. Thank you, Mr. Chairman.

---

[39] Ibid.

[40] Ibid.

[41] *http://homeland.house.gov/sites/homeland.house.gov/files/Testimony%20Joscelyn\O.pdf*

[42] Michelle Shephard, "Star Exclusive: Documents found on body of Al Qaeda's African leader detail chilling plans for kidnapping, attacks," *The Toronto Star*, July 11, 2012; (*http://www.thestar.com/news/world/2012/07/11/star\exclusive\documents\found\on\body\-of\al\qaedas\african\leader\detail\chilling\plans\for\kid-   napping\attacks.html*).

[43] "London 'sleeper cell' told to carry out wave of terror attacks by Bin Laden before his death," *The Daily Mail* (UK), May 15, 2011; (*http://www.dailymail.co.uk/news/article-1387332/Osama-Bin-Laden-dead-London-sleeper-cell-told-carry-attacks-death.html*).

[44] *http://homeland.house.gov/sites/homeland.house.gov/files/Testimony%20Joscelyn\T30.-pdf.*

[45] Bill Roggio and Thomas Joscelyn, "AQAP's emir also serves as al-Qaeda's general manager," *The Long War Journal*, August 6, 2013; (*http://www.longwarjournal.org/archives/2013/08/aqap\emir\also\serve.php*).

[46] *http://www.longwarjournal.org/images/al-qaida-papers-how-to-run-a-state.pdf.*

Thank you, Mr. Higgins, and other Members of the sub-committee, and Ms. Wilson. Let me add my thanks to those of my fellows here for the opportunity to testify.

My testimony focuses on comparing al-Qaeda and the Islamic State, with some emphasis on Africa. Two things I would like to leave you with.

One is that as rightly concerned as we are about the Islamic State, there is one person who is more concerned, and that is Ayman al-Zawahiri. This is a fundamental fight within the jihadist movement, and it is causing huge problems for them, as well.

The second is that the Islamic State poses a very serious threat, but the threat is primarily regional and to U.S. interests in the region, while al-Qaeda and the core still aims, as a primary goal, to attack the U.S. homeland.

The Islamic State evolved out of civil war, and civil wars in Iraq and Syria in particular, and its tactics reflect this. It seeks to conquer.

So if you look at how it is armed, it uses artillery, it uses mass forces, it even uses tanks and MANPADS. It sweeps into new areas with its army and it tries to defend them and then expand.

When it uses terrorism in this context, it is usually part of revolutionary war. It is trying to undermine support for the state; it is trying to destroy morale in the police forces; it is trying to create a sectarian backlash; it is trying to use terrorism to further its goals regionally.

A lot of its activities—at least the ones that I think we find most important—are part of its rather twisted model of governance. So this is rape, this is beheading, this is the use of symbolic crucifixions. It does this, in its eyes, to purify the community.

This is something that Ayman Zawahiri a decade ago, he chastised Iraqi jihadists for exactly this sort of brutality. He said it is going to backfire.

Somewhat incredibly, the Islamic State's lesson from Iraq was that they weren't brutal enough. From their point of view, controlling territory is the key. It is the key ideologically; you can't have a caliphate without it. It inspires others.

But also, its strategy is to build on this territory and expand. It is a very different model from al-Qaeda.

Both of them care about expansion, though, outside their core areas. After 9/11 al-Qaeda began to create affiliates and to forge alliances with existing groups, and now the Islamic State is playing this game. Wherever there is a call to jihad there is a rivalry, so we see this in Afghanistan and Algeria, we see it in Libya, we see it in Pakistan, Sinai, Yemen.

Al-Qaeda affiliates have actually done rather well in recent months, it is worth pointing out. In Yemen they have been taking advantage of the chaos there. In Syria we have recently seen a relatively major advance by al-Qaeda's affiliate, Jabhat al-Nusra.

But the Islamic State has gained support from a number of important groups, especially in Africa: Boko Haram, Ansar Bayt al-Maqdis in Egypt. Also, it recognized in March 2015 several provinces, including in Libya, where the Islamic State has devoted considerable resources. It is still unclear what it exactly means to be an Islamic State province.

When you were an al-Qaeda affiliate, usually it meant you shifted primarily from local attacks to ones that involved Western or international attacks in your region, as well as a more regional emphasis. Only one, al-Qaeda in the Arabian Peninsula, prioritized attacks on the United States.

The Islamic State's focus remains the Muslim world, and by taking on this label, groups seem to want the—for lack of a better term, the kind of sexiness of the Islamic State brand. It is exciting and dynamic, and they want to bring it.

Now, for now the momentum is on the Islamic State's side. It looks like a winner, and it is taking on what it considers apostates, which is a very popular trend within the broader jihadist movement. It is presenting an image of Islamic government that al-Qaeda can't match.

But the Islamic State's success is tied to its fate in Iraq and Syria. It is tied to the Islamic State, and if it suffers significant battlefield reverses, its reputation, its image will be significantly hurt.

The good news is that for now, at least—and I stress for now—the Islamic State has not actively targeted the U.S. homeland. Its emphasis has been on consolidating its state, so when it wants foreigners, it wants them to come and fight for it.

It emphasizes its role in the Muslim world, and Western security services have been on very high alert to this. They are not going to be caught napping. That doesn't mean they will be perfect, but it is not going to be a surprise.

The bad news is that a lot of the Islamic State's effect has been the Muslim world—worsening sectarianism there. There is a significant chance that there will be some young men, in particular, inspired by the Islamic State who do lone-wolf attacks. They might have never met a real Islamic State member, but they might nevertheless attack because they are inspired by it.

I will emphasize just in closing the importance of military efforts for both the drone campaign against al-Qaeda and the broader military campaign against the Islamic State to diminish its appeal.

I will share the remarks of others that the threat to U.S. personnel overseas is considerable. I don't think the threat level has changed, but I think the likelihood of a particularly gruesome death has grown because of how the Islamic State fights, and that has political ramifications.

I will stress that there is a need to resource intelligence services because this is a growing and metastasizing threat, and one that needs considerable attention.

Thank you very much.

[The prepared statement of Mr. Byman follows:]

PREPARED STATEMENT OF DANIEL BYMAN

Chairman King, Ranking Member Higgins, distinguished Members of the subcommittee, and subcommittee staff, thank you for the opportunity to testify today.

The Islamic State's influence and model are spreading. Even in many Muslim countries where the Islamic State does not have a strong presence, its rise is radicalizing their populations, fomenting sectarianism, and making a troubled region worse.[1] The Islamic State's successes in Syria and Iraq alarmed many observers in Washington and prompted the Obama administration to overcome its long-standing hesitation to become more militarily involved in Iraq and Syria. But there is one person for whom the Islamic State's rise is even more frightening: Ayman al-Zawahiri. Although the al-Qaeda leader might be expected to rejoice at the emergence of a strong jihadist group that delights in beheading Americans (among other horrors), in reality the Islamic State's rise risks al-Qaeda's demise. When Islamic State leader Abu Bakr al-Baghdadi rejected al-Qaeda's authority and later declared a caliphate, he split the always-fractious jihadist movement. The two are now competing for more than the leadership of the jihadist movement: They are competing for its soul.

Who will emerge triumphant is not clear. However, the implications of one side's victory or of continuing division are profound for the Muslim world and for the United States, shaping the likely targets of the jihadist movement, its ability to achieve its goals, and the overall stability of the Middle East. The United States can exploit this split, both to decrease the threat and to weaken the movement as a whole.

My testimony today will focus on comparing al-Qaeda and the Islamic State. I argue that al-Qaeda and its affiliates remain a threat to the U.S. homeland, while the Islamic State's danger is more to the stability of the Middle East and U.S. interests overseas. Much of their rivalry involves a competition for affiliates, with both trying to spread their model and in al-Qaeda's case to ensure its operational relevance. For now the Islamic State's focus is primarily on Iraq and Syria and to a lesser degree on other states in the Muslim world, particularly Libya. In the United States and in Europe it may inspire "lone wolves," but it is not directing its resources to attack in these areas, and security services are prepared for the threat. Al-Qaeda is weaker and less dynamic than the Islamic State, but the former remains more focused on attacking the United States and its Western allies.

My testimony is organized into four sections. I first offer some general background on the origins of al-Qaeda and the Islamic State. I then discuss the threat profiles for each group, assessing both their strategies and tactics. The third section looks at the struggle to win over affiliate groups in the Muslim world. I conclude my testimony by discussing the policy implications and recommendations for the United States.

THE DIVERSE ORIGINS OF AL-QAEDA AND THE ISLAMIC STATE

Al-Qaeda emerged out of the anti-Soviet jihad in Afghanistan in the 1980s. As the Soviets prepared to withdraw, Osama bin Laden and a few of his close associates—high on their perceived victory over the mighty Soviet Union—decided to capitalize on the network they had built to take jihad global. Bin Laden's vision was to create a vanguard of elite fighters who could lead the global jihad project and bring together the hundreds of small jihadist groups struggling, often feebly, against their own regimes under a single umbrella. By the mid-1990s, he wanted to reorient the movement as a whole, focusing it on what he saw as the bigger enemy underwriting all these corrupt local regimes: The United States. For local jihadists, pledging allegiance to bin Laden and adopting the al-Qaeda brand meant obtaining access to a wide range of assets: Money, weapons, logistical support, expertise, and, of course, training—al-Qaeda training camps were the Ivy Leagues of jihadist education.

The 1998 attacks on two U.S. embassies in Africa, and of course 9/11, made al-Qaeda's brand a household name. The attacks demonstrated the power, capabilities, reach, and sheer audacity of the organization. But although the 9/11 attacks electrified the global jihadist movement and raised al-Qaeda's profile on the global stage, the U.S. counterterrorism response that followed was devastating to both al-Qaeda and the broader movement it purported to lead. Over the next decade, the United States relentlessly pursued al-Qaeda, targeting its leadership, disrupting its finances, destroying its training camps, infiltrating its communications networks, and ultimately crippling its ability to function. It remained a symbol of the global jihadist movement, but its inability to successfully launch another major attack against the United States meant that symbol was becoming less powerful. The death of the charismatic bin Laden and the ascension of the much less compelling Ayman al-Zawahiri to the top leadership position further diminished the power of the al-Qaeda brand.

[1] This testimony draws heavily on my work with Jennifer R. Williams, particularly "ISIS vs. al-Qaeda: Jihadism's Global Civil War," *The National Interest* (February/March 2015), *http://nationalinterest.org/feature/isis-vs-al-qaeda-jihadism%E2%80%99s-global-civil-war-12304*, and my forthcoming book, *al-Qaeda, the Islamic State, and the Global Jihadist Movement: What Everyone Needs to Know* (Oxford, 2015).

The Islamic State began as an Iraqi organization, and this legacy shapes the movement today. Jihadist groups proliferated in Iraq after the 2003 U.S. invasion, and many eventually coalesced around Abu Musab al-Zarqawi, a Jordanian jihadist who spent time in Afghanistan in the 1990s and again in 2001. Though bin Laden gave Zarqawi seed money to start his organization, Zarqawi at first refused to swear loyalty to and join al-Qaeda, as he shared only some of bin Laden's goals and wanted to remain independent. After months of negotiations, however, Zarqawi pledged his loyalty, and in 2004 his group took on the name "al-Qaeda in Iraq" to signify this connection. Bin Laden got an affiliate in the most important theater of jihad at a time when the al-Qaeda core was on the ropes, and Zarqawi got al-Qaeda's prestige and contacts to bolster his legitimacy.

Yet even in its early days the group bickered with the al-Qaeda leadership. Zawahiri and bin Laden pushed for a focus on U.S. targets while Zarqawi (and those who took his place after his death in 2006 from a U.S. air strike) emphasized sectarian war and attacks on Sunni Muslims deemed apostates, such as those who collaborated with the Shi'a-led regime. Zarqawi and his followers also acted with incredible brutality, making their name with gruesome beheading videos—a tactic that its successor organizations would also use to shock and generate publicity. Zarqawi also kept his focus on Iraq and its immediate environs. Despite the fears of U.S. and European security officials, Iraq did not prove an Afghanistan-like incubator for attacks on the U.S. homeland and the West.

Al-Qaeda in Iraq's indiscriminate violence—including against its fellow Sunnis—eventually led to a backlash from the Sunni tribes that, when combined with the 2006 U.S. troop "surge" in Iraq, hit the group hard. For al-Qaeda, this was a broader disaster, with the Iraqi group's setbacks and abuses tarnishing the overall jihadist cause. Indeed, in private, al-Qaeda spokesman Adam Gadahn recommended to bin Laden that al-Qaeda publicly "sever its ties" with al-Qaeda in Iraq because of the group's sectarian violence.

When the Syria conflict broke out in 2011 and electrified the Muslim world, Zawahiri urged Iraqi jihadists to take part in the conflict, and Baghdadi—who had taken over leadership of the Iraqi group in 2010—initially sent small numbers of fighters into Syria to build an organization. Syria was in chaos, and the Iraqi jihadists established secure bases of operations there, raising money and winning new recruits to their cause. Their ambitions grew along with their organization, expanding to include Syria as well as Iraq. Iraqi jihadists, by 2013 calling themselves the Islamic State of Iraq and Syria (ISIS or ISIL) to reflect their new, broader orientation, also faced less pressure in Iraq with the departure of U.S. forces at the end of 2011. In Syria, the group took over swaths of territory, benefiting as the Syrian regime focused on more moderate groups while the Syrian opposition as a whole remained fractious. At the same time, Iraqi prime minister Nouri al-Maliki put in place a series of disastrous policies to bolster support among his Shi'a base, systematically excluding Iraqi Sunnis from power. Thus Baghdadi's organization steadily shored up popular support, regained its legitimacy in Iraq, built a base in Syria, and replenished its ranks.

Although the Syria conflict revived the Iraqi jihadist movement, it also eventually led it to split with the al-Qaeda leadership. Zawahiri encouraged the Iraqi affiliate to move into Syria, but he also wanted to establish a separate group under separate command, with Syrians in the lead to give it a local face. Zawahiri probably also wanted a separate group given his past doubts on AQI's loyalty and wisdom. Jabhat al-Nusra was thus created as the Syrian spin-off. But whereas Zawahiri saw this as a positive development, Baghdadi and other Iraqi leaders feared the group had simply gone native and become too independent, focusing too much on Syria and ignoring Iraq and the original leadership. In an attempt to rein it in and reestablish Iraqi authority over the group, Baghdadi declared Jabhat al-Nusra part of his organization. Nusra leaders balked, pledging a direct oath to Zawahiri as a way of retaining its independence. Zawahiri found this lack of unity frustrating and in late 2013 ordered Baghdadi to accept this decision and focus on Iraq. Baghdadi refused, and declared Jabhat al-Nusra subordinate to him: A move that sparked a broader clash in which thoughts of fighters from both groups died. In February of 2014, Zawahiri publicly disavowed Baghdadi's group, formally ending their affiliation.

In June 2014, Baghdadi's forces shocked just about everyone when they swept across Iraq, capturing not only large parts of Iraq's remote areas but also major cities like Mosul and Tikrit, important resources like hydroelectric dams and oil refineries, and several strategic border crossings with Syria. Within a month, the group—now calling itself the Islamic State—would officially declare the establishment of a caliphate in the territory under its control, naming Baghdadi the caliph and "leader for Muslims everywhere."[2] Almost overnight, Baghdadi went from being an annoying thorn in Zawahiri's side to a serious challenger to his authority and a threat to his organization's position as the vanguard of the global jihadist movement. Thousands more foreign fighters, inspired by the stunning success of the Islamic State and the bold declaration of a caliphate, flocked to Syria and Iraq to join the fight.

DIFFERING THREAT PROFILES

The dispute between the Islamic State and al-Qaeda is more than just a fight for power within the jihadist movement. The two organizations differ on the main enemies, strategies, tactics, and other fundamental concerns. As a result, the threat they pose to the United States differs as well.

Although the ultimate goal of al-Qaeda is to overthrow the corrupt "apostate" regimes in the Middle East and replace them with "true" Islamic governments, al-Qaeda's primary enemy is the United States, which it sees as the root cause of the Middle East's problems. By targeting the United States, al-Qaeda believes it will eventually induce the United States to end support for these Muslim state regimes and withdraw from the region altogether, thus leaving the regimes vulnerable to attack from within. Al-Qaeda considers Shi'a Muslims to be apostates but sees their killing to be too extreme, a waste of resources, and detrimental to the broader jihadist project. Yet Zawahiri cannot openly oppose sectarianism: It is too popular, and with the sectarian slaughter in the Syrian civil war, too many in the Muslim world find it compelling.

The Islamic State does not follow al-Qaeda's "far enemy" strategy, preferring instead the "near enemy" strategy, albeit on a regional level. As such, the primary target of the Islamic State has not been the United States, but rather "apostate" regimes in the Arab world—namely, the Asad regime in Syria and the Abadi regime in Iraq. Like his predecessors, Baghdadi favors purifying the Islamic community first by attacking Shi'a and other religious minorities as well as rival jihadist groups. The Islamic State's long list of enemies includes the Iraqi Shi'a, the Lebanese Hizballah, the Yazidis (a Kurdish ethno-religious minority located predominantly in Iraq), and rival opposition groups in Syria (including Jabhat al-Nusra, the official al-Qaeda affiliate in Syria).

Ostensibly in response to intervention by the United States and others in the conflict, Western civilians in the region (including journalists and humanitarian aid workers) have also become targets—though the Islamic State saw them as hostile before the U.S. intervention. And now that American military advisers are on the ground in Iraq supporting the Iraqi military, the U.S. military has ostensibly become a primary target for the Islamic State, but the lack of troops within range diminishes this danger.

Al-Qaeda has long used a mix of strategies to achieve its objectives. To fight the United States, al-Qaeda plots terrorism spectaculars to electrify the Muslim world (and get it to follow al-Qaeda's banner) and to convince the United States to retreat from the Muslim world: The model is based on the U.S. withdrawals from Lebanon after Hizballah bombed the Marine barracks and U.S. embassy there and the "Blackhawk Down" incident in Somalia. In addition, al-Qaeda supports insurgents in the Islamic world to fight against U.S.-backed regimes (and U.S. forces in places like Afghanistan, where it hopes to replicate the Soviet experience). Finally, al-Qaeda issues a swarm of propaganda to convince Muslims that jihad is their obligation and to convince jihadists to adopt al-Qaeda's goals over their local ones.

The Islamic State embraces some of these goals, but even where there is agreement in principle, its approach is quite different. The Islamic State's strategy is to control territory, steadily consolidating and expanding its position. Part of this is ideological: It wants to create a government where Muslims can live under Islamic law (or the Islamic State's twisted version of it). Part of this is inspirational: By creating an Islamic state, it electrifies many Muslims who then embrace the group. And part of it is basic strategy: By controlling territory it can build an army, and by using its army it can control more territory.

The two groups' preferred tactics reflect these strategic differences. Al-Qaeda has long favored large-scale, dramatic attacks against strategic or symbolic targets: The attacks on the World Trade Center and the Pentagon on 9/11 are the most prominent, but the 1998 bombings of the U.S. embassies in Kenya and Tanzania, the attack on U.S.S. Cole in the port of Aden in 2000, and plots like the 2005 attempt to down over 10 transatlantic flights all show an emphasis on the spectacular. At

---

[2] "ISIS jihadists declare 'Islamic caliphate'," *Al Arabiya*, June 29, 2014, *http://english.alarabiya.net/en/News/2014/06/29/ISIS-jihadists-declare-caliphate-.html*.

the same time, al-Qaeda has backed an array of lesser terrorist attacks on Western, Jewish, and other enemy targets; trained insurgents; and otherwise tried to build guerrilla armies.

Yet although al-Qaeda has repeatedly called for attacks against Westerners, and especially Americans, it has refrained from killing Westerners when it suited its purposes. Perhaps the most notable example of this is found in al-Qaeda's decision on multiple occasions to grant Western journalists safe passage into al-Qaeda safe havens and allow them to interview bin Laden face-to-face. Terrorism doesn't work if no one is watching, and in the days before YouTube and Twitter, al-Qaeda needed Western journalists to bring its message to its target audience. Al-Qaeda often takes a similar approach to Western aid workers operating in its midst: On at least two occasions, senior leaders of the al-Qaeda-linked Jabhat al-Nusra implored the Islamic State to release Western aid workers the Islamic State had captured and were threatening to execute. The leaders of the al-Qaeda affiliate argued that Alan Henning and later Peter Kassig were innocent aid workers who were risking their lives to help ease the suffering of Muslims in Syria and that kidnapping and executing them was "wrong under Islamic law" and "counter-productive."[3] Unfortunately, the Islamic State was not swayed by such arguments, and both men were horrifically executed.

The Islamic State evolved out of the civil wars in Iraq and Syria, and its tactics reflect this context. The Islamic State seeks to conquer; thus it deploys artillery, massed forces, and even tanks and MANPADS as it sweeps into new areas or defends existing holdings. Terrorism, in this context, is part of revolutionary war: It is used to undermine morale in the army and police, force a sectarian backlash, or otherwise create dynamics that help conquest on the ground. But it is an adjunct to a more conventional struggle.

In territory it controls, the Islamic State uses mass executions, public beheadings, rape, and symbolic crucifixion displays to terrorize the population into submission and "purify" the community, and at the same time provides basic (if minimal) services: The mix earns them some support, or at least acquiescence due to fear, from the population. Al-Qaeda, in contrast, favors a more gentle approach. A decade ago Zawahiri chastised the Iraqi jihadists for their brutality, correctly believing this would turn the population against them and alienate the broader Muslim community, and he has raised this issue in the current conflict as well. Al-Qaeda recommends proselytizing in the parts of Syria where its affiliate Jabhat al-Nusra holds sway, trying to convince local Muslims to adopt al-Qaeda's views rather than forcing them to do so. The Islamic State's lesson from Iraq, somewhat incredibly, is that it was not brutal enough.

THE FIGHT FOR AFFILIATES

Al-Qaeda and the Islamic State both profess to lead the jihadist cause throughout the Muslim world. After 9/11, al-Qaeda began to create affiliates or forge alliances with existing groups, expanding its range but at the same time exposing its brand to the misdeeds of local groups, as happened in Iraq.[4] As part of its competition with the Islamic State, al-Qaeda has stepped up affiliation, establishing relationships with groups in the Caucasus, Tunisia, and India. The Islamic State is playing this game too, and wherever there is a call to jihad, there is a rivalry. Afghanistan, Algeria, Libya, Pakistan, Sinai, Yemen, and other Muslim lands are part of the competition.

Although attention is focused on the Islamic State, al-Qaeda affiliates have done well in recent months.[5] In Yemen, AQAP has exploited the chaos there to take terri-

---

[3] Tom Harper, "Alan Henning: Al-Qaeda appealed to Isis to release British aid worker following kidnap," *The Independent*, April 22, 2015, *http://www.independent.co.uk/news/world/middle-east/alan-henning-alqaeda-appealed-to-isis-to-release-british-aid-worker-following-kidnap-9734598.html*; Ruth Sherlock and Richard Spencer, "Senior al-Qaeda jihadist speaks out in defence of Peter Kassig," *The Telegraph*, October 22, 2014, *http://www.telegraph.co.uk/news/worldnews/islamic-state/11181229/Senior-al-Qaeda-jihadist-speaks-out-in-defence-of-Peter-Kassig.html*. The case of Peter Kassig was especially controversial, as it seems Kassig may have actually personally provided emergency medical care to Abu Omar Acidi, the Jabhat al-Nusra leader who called on the Islamic State to release Kassig, as well as several other jihadists, and because Kassig had converted to Islam during his time working in Syria.

[4] For more on affiliates and al-Qaeda, see Daniel Byman, "Breaking the Bonds between Al-Qa'ida and Its Affiliate Organizations" (Brookings, 2012) *http://www.brookings.edu//media/research/files/papers/2012/7/alqaida%20terrorism%20byman/alqaida%20terrorism%20byman.pdf*.

[5] For a nice review, see Daveed Gartenstein-Ross and Bridget Moreng, "al-Qaeda Is Beating the Islamic State," *Politico*, April 14, 2015.

tory, freeing imprisoned militants and seizing arms. In Syria, al-Qaeda's affiliate Jabhat al-Nusra has cooperated with other groups to take Idlib, an important advance, as well as other gains.

The Islamic State has gained support from a number of important jihadist groups. Boko Haram in Nigeria and Ansar Bayt al-Maqdis in Egypt both formally pledged allegiance to the Islamic State and are now considered official affiliates or "provinces" of the Islamic State; as of March 2015, the Islamic State has formally recognized seven provinces, including in Libya, from whence many of its foreign fighters hail, and in Yemen, where it is now in direct competition with al-Qaeda in the Arabian Peninsula (AQAP). In March, Islamic State supporters in Yemen bombed Houthi mosques, playing on the sectarian war narrative that the Islamic State has long emphasized and al-Qaeda has long sought to suppress—indeed, AQAP immediately issued a statement publicly disavowing any involvement in the mosque bombings. It is difficult, however, to gauge the overall level of Islamic State support. Al-Qaeda has historically been fairly quiet for a terrorist group when it comes to claiming and boasting of attacks, while the Islamic State often exaggerates its own prowess and role to the point of absurdity.

What becoming an Islamic State "province" means in practice is difficult to determine. In the past, when an affiliate joined al-Qaeda, it usually took on more regional activities and went after more international targets in its region, but did not focus on attacks in the West. Only one affiliate—AQAP—prioritized striking the U.S. homeland and Europe. The Islamic State's focus remains expansion in the Muslim world, and for now its affiliates are likely to focus there. By taking on the Islamic State label, local groups seem to want to attach themselves to a brand that has caught the attention of jihadists world-wide. They are more likely to embrace the Islamic State's barbarous tactics like beheadings as well as its sectarian orientation. In Afghanistan and Yemen, Islamic State-oriented groups have brutally attacked these countries' Shi'a.

POLICY IMPLICATIONS AND RECOMMENDATIONS

For now the momentum is on the Islamic State's side. Unlike al-Qaeda, it looks like a winner: Triumphant in Iraq and Syria, taking on the Shi'a apostates and even the United States at a local level, and presenting a vision of Islamic governance that al-Qaeda cannot match. Yet this ascendance may be transitory. The Islamic State's fate is tied to Iraq and Syria, and reverses on the battlefield—more likely now that the United States and its allies are more engaged—could over time reduce its appeal. Like its predecessor organization in Iraq, the Islamic State may also find that its brutality repels more than it attracts, diminishing its luster among potential supporters and making it vulnerable when the people suddenly turn against it.

However, the Islamic State's triumphs so far have profound implications for U.S. counterterrorism. The good news is that the Islamic State is not targeting the American homeland—at least for now. Its emphasis is on consolidating and expanding its state, and even the many foreign fighters who have flocked to its banner are being used in suicide bombings or other attacks on its immediate enemies, not on plots back in the West. Western security services are on high alert against the Islamic State threat.

The bad news is that the Islamic State is far more successful in achieving its goals than al-Qaeda has been: Like it or not, the Islamic State really is a "state" in that it controls territory and governs it. Its military presence is roiling Iraq and Syria and the threat it poses extends to Jordan, Saudi Arabia, Egypt, Libya, Yemen, and especially Lebanon. The thousands of foreign fighters under its banner are post a risk of greater regional instability at the very least, and U.S. officials legitimately fear they pose a counterterrorism problem for the West. Ideologically, the sectarianism it foments is worsening Shi'a-Sunni tension throughout the region. So the Islamic State is a much bigger threat to Middle East stability than al-Qaeda ever was.

The Islamic State's impressive social media efforts and overall appeal also make it better able to mobilize "lone wolves" to attack in the West. Many of these individuals will have had little or no contact with the Islamic State as an organization, but they find its ideology and methods appealing and will act on their own. Ironically, some of these individuals may have preferred to go to Iraq and Syria, but Western disruption efforts make it easier for them to attack at home.

The United States and its allies should try to exploit the fight between the Islamic State and al-Qaeda and, ideally, diminish them both. The infighting goes against what either organization claims to want, and it diminishes the appeal of jihad if volunteers believe they will be fighting the jihadist down the block rather than the Asad regime, Americans, Shi'a, or other enemies. Efforts to stop foreign fighters should stress this infighting. The Islamic State's social media strategy is also a propaganda weakness: Because the organization allows bottom-up efforts, it risks allowing the most foolish or horrific low-level member to define the group. Playing up its atrocities, especially against other Sunni Muslims, will steadily discredit the group.

Military efforts matter tremendously beyond the immediate theater of operations. For al-Qaeda, the constant drone campaign has diminished the core in Pakistan and made it harder for it to exercise control over the broader movement. Zawahiri himself is an important target, as he is the last major figure of the original generation of al-Qaeda with a global profile, and he will not be easily replaced. For the Islamic State, defeat on the ground will do more to diminish its appeal than any propaganda measure. The Islamic State's self-proclaimed mission—establishing and expanding a caliphate—is also a vulnerability. If it fails at this mission by losing territory, its luster will diminish.

The threat to U.S. personnel overseas near conflict zones remains high. Al-Qaeda, its affiliates, and local jihadist groups have long put them in their crosshairs, and the Islamic State is likely to do the same. The overall level of risk remains roughly similar, but their manner of death if captured is likely to be more gruesome at the hands of the Islamic State.

Because of the appeal and strength of both al-Qaeda affiliates and the Islamic State, programs to gather intelligence and develop the strength of local regimes (and at times substate groups when the regime is weak or hostile as in the case of Syria) are vital. These must be properly resourced and bureaucratically prioritized. At times U.S. personnel must be deployed in dangerous areas, taking on considerable risk. Particularly important is identifying potential areas of expansion for jihadist groups and working with allies to exert control, nipping problems in the bud. Nigeria, Libya, and Yemen are only a few countries where the problems steadily grew worse but attracted only limited U.S. attention. Because the quality of government matters as well as the amount of control a government exerts, the United States should also encourage political reform in such countries.

Some degree of continued infighting between al-Qaeda and the Islamic State is the most likely outcome. As such, the United States should prepare to confront a divided adversary. The good news is that the fight within may consume most of our adversary's attention; the bad news is that anti-U.S. violence or high-profile attacks in the Middle East may become more intense as each side seeks to outmatch its rival. Yet while spikes in violence may occur, such infighting will undermine their ability to shape regional politics, diminish both movements' overall influence, and ultimately discredit jihadism in general.

Mr. KING. Doctor, thank you very much.

I will begin my questioning.

Mr. Joscelyn, in your testimony—I would ask the other two witnesses to comment, as well—you basically spoke of the directive that bin Laden had imposed on al-Qaeda affiliates in Africa to attack the United States, be ready to carry out external attacks. With bin Laden gone, even though that may still be al-Qaeda policy, do you feel it is as strictly enforced or expected as much now as it was under bin Laden?

Mr. JOSCELYN. Well, I will say this: Al-Qaeda has always been able to walk and chew gum at the same time. They have always had some small part of the resources devoted to coming after us while actually, if you investigate them throughout their whole history back to when—right through the founding, they devoted most of the resources to insurgency warfare, including the training in pre-9/11 Afghanistan.

So they are always trying to spread their base, basically, across the globe. What I would say that has changed is that since bin Laden was killed, they have had more opportunities for that insurgency type of warfare, as Dr. Byman mentioned.

It had some pretty stunning gains in Syria of late. But you can also see some areas in Africa where they have gained and, of course, in Yemen.

I guess my message is that as their insurgency base spreads, we have a lot of historical examples that would also spread through that as a potential threat to us, because everywhere they go there is some part of their operation which is going to be devoted to coming after U.S. interests abroad and potentially against the U.S. homeland.

I don't think that has changed under Ayman al-Zawahiri in his leadership of al-Qaeda. I think he was in lockstep—in fact, you can see in the bin Laden files he basically agrees with the whole strategy all along. So I think it is sort of the same modus operandi today.

Mr. KING. Dr. Pham.

Mr. PHAM. Mr. Chairman, I would agree with my friend, Mr. Joscelyn, and then just simply add the evidence is there with the groups that are affiliated with al-Qaeda. You have, for example, Shabaab—much has been made by some in the administration and others about the great successes defeating al-Shabaab in the so-called Somali model when in actuality, the military defeats were an inadvertent favor to the more radical leadership of Shabaab, which could now, freed from the constraints of having to govern parochial concerns within Somalia, have actually grown in their virulence as transnational groups.

Just on the matter of al-Shabaab, I would cite the fact that between the Westgate attack in September 2013 and the Garissa University College attack this month, largely unreported in the Western media were some—more than 60 attacks with more than 400 victims. So these attacks are increasing, and one could say the same about al-Qaeda in the Islamic Maghreb, its splinter groups, et cetera. So the virulence certainly continues, sir.

Mr. KING. Dr. Byman.

Mr. BYMAN. What I would stress, sir, is that I think the intention to attack the U.S. homeland remains strong, but the al-Qaeda core's capabilities have been hurt quite a bit. Several things—I mentioned the drone campaign. It makes it very hard for them to do command and control.

Their leaders have to be hiding. There is a reason we haven't heard from Zawahiri in quite some time, and I think it is very hard for them to kind of exercise a global leadership the way they have in the past.

Also, the intelligence liaison efforts are much stronger, and so there is coordination around the world. I don't want to say this is perfect, but if you look at, for example, the Charlie Hebdo attacks in Paris, one of the successes buried in this really horrible event was that U.S. intelligence was warning French intelligence about several of these individuals, saying that there was a Yemen connection. That is a tribute to the resources and the skill of the people involved.

So my sense is that while Zawahiri would like nothing better than a high-profile attack on the United States, his desire has not led to success because of some significant blows his organization has taken.

Mr. KING. I have one question for each of you. Is there any nation state's government in Africa that you would say is likely to either collapse or be overrun or compromised by Islamic terrorists?

I will start with Dr. Pham.

Mr. PHAM. Certainly one could already write off Libya as certainly a collapsed state, but on-going—right now we pretend, if you will, that we have a government in Somalia. In reality, we don't have a government.

They never take quorum calls at the parliament because if they did they never could legally meet. So we pretend there is a government and, in fact, that hampers on a number of levels our ability to effectively deal with challenges there. So that is a collapsed government that we pretend is otherwise.

I think the governments of the Sahel are very, very marginal. Again, we pretend there is a government in the Central African Republic, but that is a witch's brew.

Chad, long-time dictator. It has contributed to the fight against Boko Haram, but on very brittle foundations. Niger is a democracy, a good ally, but they are in an impossible neighborhood, sandwiched between al-Qaeda in the Islamic Maghreb and other groups in Mali, the remnants of Boko Haram in Nigeria and Libya and Algeria, desperately in need of cooperation and assistance from us.

Mali remains very fragile. The French staved off collapse by the intervention in 2013, but two-thirds of the country still are no-go zones and there are attacks on the U.N. peacekeepers today. So that region is entirely volatile.

Mr. KING. Mr. Joscelyn.

Mr. JOSCELYN. Yes. I was going to start with Mali, actually. I think Mali is the place where a large portion of the country is still very destabilized and under the control of jihadists, and they basically are running—what happened with the French-led intervention is that many of the forces melted away, as opposed to being killed off by Western forces, and lived to fight another day.

So the situation there is precarious. I don't think that they are going to fall tomorrow, but there is certainly an on-going threat there.

The other country I would highlight is—and I don't think it is necessarily going to fall, but it is a fragile sort of—one of the few success stories of the Arab Spring is Tunisia, which really requires a lot of international support and is getting support from the U.S. Government against the jihadist threat, because it really is a prominent threat in that country.

Mr. KING. Dr. Byman.

Mr. BYMAN. I have nothing to add to my colleagues. I think they covered the landscape well.

Mr. KING. Thank you.

With that, I recognize the gentleman from New York, the Ranking Member.

Mr. HIGGINS. Thank you, Mr. Chairman.

Al-Shabaab has demonstrated success in bombing urban centers, primarily in East Africa. Yet, the United States has a pretty significant Somali population. How likely is it that there would be a coordinated or lone-wolf attack on the American homeland by al-Shabaab?

Mr. JOSCELYN. I will say, you know, I can't say exactly how likely it is; it is always a possibility. I would say that the FBI and other

U.S. Government services are obviously spending a lot of time trying to neutralize that possibility and counter it.

But again, you know, I think one of the big things here messaging-wise is to understand that even the Somali community in Minnesota and elsewhere, they have been victimized by this, as well. Highlighting that and understanding that these guys who go off to fight for Shabaab are primarily going to kill Muslims in Somalia or Africans, and not U.S. forces, not Western forces, is a very strong, powerful message to sort of act as a deterrent for that sort of thing back here at home.

In other words, you are not going to be celebrated as a hero; you are going to be celebrated as part of this violent ideology, which is killing, supposedly, your own kind.

Mr. PHAM. I would just add to that. The overwhelming majority, clearly, of Somali-Americans are opposed to this ideology and opposed to this violence. But the one thing about Shabaab that bears recalling, it is one of the few of the groups that we have discussed today that has shown consistently over time an ability to attract however small a minority and isolated group throughout a community—not just lone wolves, but networks of people.

The arrests just a little over a week ago of six Somali-Americans who were headed to the Islamic State, these were the same networks that sent people to al-Shabaab just a few years ago. So there is an organic network, and the convictions and prosecutions by Department of Justice and other law enforcement just underscores that there is, however, within a small minority, this group an organic network.

Mr. BYMAN. At the risk of being seen as naive, I am actually a bit more optimistic on this question, I think, than many people. There is always a danger of lone wolves when you have a kind of broader jihadist mindset, but the people who have gone to Somalia so far we have not seen a strong desire of those going there to return and fight. What they have been trying to do is fight in Somalia and at times in the region.

That is the cause; they have seen it as legitimate.

There was a strong kind of anger at the United States a decade ago when this began because the United States was seen as secretly behind the Ethiopian invasion. That is not the focus today of the people going.

So there is, again, a desire to go and fight, but it is not rooted in anti-Americanism. There will be some who return. Some of those will be radicalized. But so far, the FBI in particular has shown that they have these networks reasonably well penetrated.

Mr. KING. Gentleman yields back.

The gentleman from Pennsylvania, Mr. Barletta.

Mr. BARLETTA. Thank you, Mr. Chairman.

Dr. Pham, we know from the 9/11 Commission that terrorists want two things: To find a way to enter the United States, and then to stay here. While recognizing the humanitarian crisis in areas ravaged by the Islamic State and overrun by al-Qaeda, we must also not forget that there are those that wish to do us harm and must, therefore, remain vigilant as to who we admit into the United States.

Just this February FBI Assistant Director Michael Steinbach testified before the full Homeland Security Committee and expressed concern as to whether our Government has sufficient intelligence in Syria to properly vet potential refugees from that state. In your experience, does the United States have adequate intelligence to properly vet refugees applying from areas within Africa where al-Qaeda and the Islamic State are present and active?

Mr. PHAM. My experience is that our embassies in Africa as a whole are very under-resourced. The process for review of visas is very often—they try their best; I am not going to—but the flood of applications versus what they have to process and the turnaround times, I know—I frequently hear from Foreign Service officers as well as people detailed from other Government agencies, as well as, often cases—some embassies spouses of Foreign Service officers are employed on temporary contracts just to process things. So the answer, sir, is, unfortunately, no.

Mr. BARLETTA. Does the new alliance between Boko Haram and the Islamic State complicate United States intelligence-gathering efforts in that region?

Mr. PHAM. Well, our intelligence efforts in Nigeria have been riddled with complications and difficulties really for quite some time. Part of it was relationships with the Nigerian government itself. Part of it is simply lack of resources.

Just to give you an example, Nigeria is a country, sir, of, as you know, almost 180 million people. Yet, we have no diplomatic presence north of the capital of Abuja. So quite simply, we don't have the eyes and ears on the ground.

Repeatedly, I think it is in the legislation—the foreign opps bill, once again to study placing a consulate in northern Nigeria, which would then become a base for reporting. But quite simply, we—large parts of Africa's most populous country are simply—we are blind to.

Mr. BARLETTA. Finally, do you have a recommendation as to how the United States can protect itself from inadvertently admitting a sympathizer or a member from al-Shabaab or Boko Haram?

Mr. PHAM. Sir, I don't have a quick fix. What I do advocate is we need to put resources across the whole—certainly in the Department of State, but also homeland security, law enforcement agencies.

Our analytical and intelligence capabilities in Africa are, quite simply, not up to the challenge that we face. That was even before sequestration.

Mr. BARLETTA. Thank you.

I yield back, Mr. Chairman.

Mr. KING. He yields back.

Does Ranking Member have a motion?

Mr. HIGGINS. Yes. Mr. Chairman, I ask unanimous consent to let the gentlewoman from Texas, Ms. Jackson Lee, be allowed to sit and question the witnesses.

Mr. KING. With some trepidation, without objection, so ordered.

Ms. JACKSON LEE. Mr. Chairman, you know that you are very glad to see me, and we have some of the mutual tendencies of compassion and passion, along with the Ranking Member. Thank you so very much for this——

Mr. KING. Also, I would like to say to the gentlelady, I know she is here today primarily over what happened in Nigeria with the girls, and I really thank you for your efforts on that.

Ms. JACKSON LEE. Thank you so very much, Mr. Chairman. I will have my line of questioning.

First of all, let me thank the witnesses who are here, and it was through this committee that I was able to lead a delegation to Africa in 2014. My colleague, Congresswoman Wilson, was very pivotal part of this. Very delighted to see her.

Would start my questioning both to Mr. Higgins and to Mr. King. Again in appreciation, and I would offer to say that this would be another important opportunity for the Homeland Security Committee, this committee, to go to Africa and pursue some of the lines of questioning and issues.

Mr. King, let me just be very clear: We are now facing what you have been speaking about for a long time, which is franchised terrorism, individuals who leave this country and go to fight in foreign fields, and then we also have continents that we would have never expected or did not have that, say, 10 years ago.

I studied in Africa, went to school in Africa, and would say to you that as I have traveled throughout the continent, I find that the larger percentage of heads of states in this era are pushing back on terrorism, but they need our help, and they need the intelligence that we have and the kind of hearings that we are having here.

I met with the chairwoman of the African Union. The African Union, in particular, has recognized that they have to have a role, and they have a military operation particularly dealing with Boko Haram in Cameroon, Niger, and Nigeria.

I met also with the former president of Nigeria, President Obasanjo, who was in contact with President Buhari, and we made the point that he cannot pull back on the fight against Boko Haram.

So I want to say to these individuals that one of the things that we have to do is to look at these countries not as a continent, but as individual countries who have their own opposition, own crisis.

I would ask Dr. Byman to follow my line of questioning on this whole question of terrorism in Africa. You have the Somalian effort—I wouldn't call it—it is too polite to call it—terrorists, if you will—who are incensed with Kenya and continue to make Kenya a target. You have the ISIL capacity and the disruption in Libya and Northern Africa, moving—when Gaddafi was alive, a lot of these countries relied upon Gaddafi's largess. Now I am not sure whether they feel oppressed and they are relying upon ISIL, which is obviously devastating.

But my question is, Boko Haram, that are, I might say, thugs and terrorists, are at the heinous and lowest vile level of treatment. Can this, in collaboration with the United States intelligence, can there be an effort waged by African countries who individually have their own sovereignty against this threat? Can a collective response come about?

Mr. BYMAN. I think we are seeing the beginnings of a collective response. Part of that is military and part of it is better information sharing. Here the United States can play a tremendous role, because often these governments don't coordinate well with each other and the United States, if you will, can be the concert master, bringing the different instruments together.

However, for Boko Haram in particular, the solutions begin and end with the Nigerian government. There may be an opportunity for improvement with the new government, but there are tremendous problems at all levels, right?

So whether these are the broader problems that lead people to join the group, whether it is the breakdown of local law and order, whether it is the distrust felt by many citizens for the government, whether it is the tremendous corruption and abuse within the military, I would say that certainly regional solutions matter and are part of this, but the primary emphasis must be on Nigeria.

Ms. JACKSON LEE. Mr. Chairman, if—I see my time is running out. Let me thank you for that.

We have focused on Nigeria. The delegation went to Nigeria, met in Abuja.

What I would say to my colleagues, you have a very eager aspect of the Africa Command. That is not the civilian part, but the African Command wants to utilize its intelligence capacity. Many of you know the Leahy provisions, which have been appreciated for what they stood for about human rights, but that is a bar for an extended utilization of intelligence.

I would hope this committee, which recognizes that anything outside of our boundaries can get into our boundaries, that we would pay a pivotal—could play a pivotal role in being demonstrative about getting ahead of this terrorist movement in Africa where heads of states want to fight against it, and to find a way to share intelligence, to find a way to share expertise, because I frankly think that the Africa Command that is on the ground now has been very helpful to the Nigerian military. We met with the Nigerian military, and these gentlemen looked proficient but needed help, and they wanted help.

So I think we can—this committee, I think, can be very helpful in making sure that the new administration does not pull away from fighting Boko Haram in particular—I know that there are a number of others—from fighting Boko Haram as Kenya is trying to fight al-Shabaab and pushing back on ISIL, but fighting them, but also not letting the heat off of them for finding those girls in Chibok, for not saying, ''We think they are married off, they have become Muslims.''

Those families are not ceding the point that their girls, who were in the school simply to take exams—Christian girls—to take exams, that they have now gone off and they have become Muslim and they are married. We don't know what is in their little minds. They may be doing things to survive, but they are not—they may not be where if you pull them out, give them and restore their lives with their families, that they would be able to do that.

I do want to make note of the fact that—excuse me, that Boko Haram is killing Christians, killing Muslims, or burning mosques, or burning hospitals, et cetera. So I think this committee—I am so grateful for this hearing, and I think this committee can be enormously great—a very—because we have a broad policy. We are not intelligence; we are broad policy.

I think this subcommittee can be a great leader in this issue, and we can get in front of this movement with leaders in—on the continent who really want to work with us, who really want to push—it doesn't help them at all. They are emerging developing nations and this terrorist threat and this terrorist huge mountain of fear does not do them any good.

To the gentleman's comment—and I will close—to the gentleman's comment, to the doctor's comment, that was one of the reasons that the northern state felt that they were not getting the resources, and in actuality, the intelligentsia started the concept of Boko Haram, but it was an intellectual discussion, peaceful, ''We are going to fight against you through words.''

Then, of course, it got pulled off. These guys got pushed to the side, and we now have this violent, heinous leader, which must be caught.

I just wanted to just double-compliment you for this. It is one of the committees that has taken this on head-on, and however I can be of help, and I would make the very large suggestion to invite—to ask you two gentlemen that we can join and lead a delegation back to the continent on these many, many issues. I think it would be a very important mission on behalf of the United States of America.

Your kindness has been very much appreciated, and with that, I yield back.

Mr. KING. Gentlelady yields back, and I thank her for her passion and dedication.

Now the gentlelady from Florida, Ms. Wilson, is recognized. Thank you for joining us today.

Ms. WILSON of Florida. Thank you, Mr. Chairman, for allowing me to join you today.

Thank you, to the Ranking Member.

Thank you, to the panel.

This is truly something that I am truly concerned about, and I just wanted to find out today how deeply the Homeland Security Committee was involved in this. I have been working with the Foreign Affairs Committee, who sponsored the trip that we took last year to Nigeria, and to hear Ms. Jackson Lee ask you to take a trip, it would—I would love to accompany you, just like we did to—with the Foreign Affairs Committee.

All of the women of the Congress, Democrats and Republicans, were asked to wear red today. We are wearing red to signify Bring Back Our Girls, and it is just so wonderful that we heard of the discovery of 300 women and girls who have been discovered, and we are not sure yet if any of the missing Chibok girls that were kidnapped during the raid on the school by Boko Haram are amongst the girls that have been discovered, so we are waiting for that intelligence to come forward.

But it just so happens that all of these women and girls were in one place, so I think the entire Congress' ears or the antennas are up, trying to hear what kind of intelligence we can get from that particular issue.

We know that ISIS, that—well, Boko Haram reached out to ISIS for partnership, and at my last readings, ISIS accepted that partnership. I am not sure if that is true or if that is propaganda by Boko Haram.

If they did accept that partnership, I would like to know what are some of the consequences that are likely to result from Boko Haram's attempt to ally itself with ISIS, and would we have advance knowledge of plans to attack Americans or carry out attacks in the United States by Boko Haram with the marriage of Boko Haram and ISIS?

Mr. PHAM. Thank you very much, Ms. Wilson, for your great interest and passion on this. To answer your question about the alliance between Boko Haram and ISIS, this is a copy, a printout of ISIS's magazine, the current issue, and it says "Shariah Alone Will Rule Africa," and there is a whole section, and they go through—lay out exactly what they expect from this alliance, and they—it is very explicit that those people who want to get—join the Islamic State and fight but because of tighter border controls and vigilance can't get across the border into Iraq or Syria or can't move on from Libya, they are encouraging them to link up with Boko Haram and fight there in their so-called Islamic State West Africa Province.

So the short answer to your factual question is that is what ISIS is calling for.

The broader answer is, how does this affect this? Very potentially, if Boko Haram—and this is a big if—maintain—manages to maintain a territorial foothold—they have been pushed out. Nigerian military and its regional allies have done a great job pushing them out. If they, however, maintain some sort of territorial foothold, then these fighters have a place to go to and then we have a serious regional issue. That is the upside for Boko Haram.

The downside is as they get farther from the local matrix in which they are embedded it becomes a little more difficult for them. So I think the jury is still out, but it is something that certainly threatens Nigeria, its neighbors, and the international security as a whole.

Ms. WILSON of Florida. Do you have any—Mr. Chairman, do you have any information or updates of anyone in the United States that are connected with Boko Haram in any way that would issue a threat for local people joining and that would carry out attacks for Boko Haram in the United States since the kidnap of the girls? Any intelligence seeping out on that area?

Mr. JOSCELYN. I will say this quickly—I don't have anything specifically on that and calling for attacks, you know, in that regard. But we are already starting to see how the Islamic State's African presence, from the Northern Africa down through Boko Haram, is starting to attract Western recruits and foreigners. In fact, there was recently there was an arrest of an American who was going to fight off for the Islamic State in Derna, Libya, and basically he and his cousin allegedly were planning—and a plot also in Illinois.

So you see the potential for this type of thing already, where, as Dr. Pham noted, when they accepted—the Islamic State accepted the Boko Haram pledge of allegiance they explicitly said they wanted foreigners and recruits from the West and elsewhere to come to West Africa if they couldn't come to the Islamic State elsewhere. So there is always that potential there for that type of thing.

Ms. WILSON of Florida. Thank you.

I see my time is up. I am concerned about the homeland, and I am concerned about Africa. But No. 1, the homeland, as to what kind of threat does Boko Haram have on the homeland, America.

Thank you.

Mr. KING. Gentlelady yields back.

In discussion with the Ranking Member, since votes are coming up we will try to limit another round to 2 minutes for each of the Members.

Mr. Joscelyn, I would like to follow up on what you just said now, because that was going to be my question, is that we focus on foreign fighters coming from Syria. That is the main focus we have had.

But now, in view of the shifting alliances or the growing alliances, and with ISIS recommending or urging that foreign fighters go to Libya, how much of a threat do you see that to the United States, for instance, foreign fighters going to other countries besides Syria, which is difficult enough to monitor, but, you know, can we see Libya, can we see other countries in Africa where those foreign fighters would go and then return to the United States or to Europe?

Mr. JOSCELYN. I think the potential is obviously greater for a return to Europe, and you can see all the European security services, intelligence services are, in some cases, very freaked out about the whole thing because they realize they have a growing problem.

But I would say, the whole issue here——

Mr. KING. But you know, you should mention, because of the visa waiver those Europeans could come to the United States unless they have been monitored.

Mr. JOSCELYN. There is a potential for that for traveling, obviously, in the United States, absolutely.

I would say the problem is really to look at it holistically. My big concern is that what is going on in North Africa isn't distinct from what is happening in Syria and Iraq. These facilitation networks have been long connected and are tied directly together. We witness on a regular basis the flow of fighters and leaders across these borders.

In fact, you know, I said in my written testimony, in fact, one of the guys who helped recruit the 9/11 hijackers actually traveled to Egypt to help broker an alliance for the Islamic State with the group in the Sinai. This is stunning.

I mean, this is a guy who was—helped recruit the 9/11 hijackers that came and attacked us here is actually traveling to North Africa and the Sinai on behalf of the Islamic State. This is the type of thing that I find to be very worrisome, because you don't know what else he could be doing.

Mr. KING. Dr. Byman, do you have any——

Mr. BYMAN. I will add both a note of bad news that is obvious, but also a note of good news.

The broader the movement spreads, the more affiliates it has, the more places that need to be monitored. The good news, though, is it is a coordination problem for the Islamic State.

There is an intelligence saying that 1 plus 1 equals 11, right, that the more you add to the circle, the more opportunities you have to discover this. So if they are trying to launch operations based in Syria via Libya then there are multiple places to learn about it and disrupt it. So it is harder for them, even though it is also challenging for us.

Mr. KING. Ranking Member is recognized for 2 minutes.

Mr. HIGGINS. Yes. Thank you, Mr. Chairman.

The former Nigerian president didn't have much of an appetite for, you know, fighting Boko Haram. What is the likely change with the new administration relative to that issue?

Mr. PHAM. The president elect, Muhammadu Buhari, is a retired military officer. He is a major general rank. The perception is that he will—he understands the military—he is a Muslim from the north of Nigeria—so that he would be able to move with more resolution.

To be fair to the out-going president, I think we have to acknowledge that the day before he lost the election was the day that the military took back Gwoza, the headquarters of Boko Haram. So a bit of progress, perhaps a bit too late both for his political fortunes, but there were some efforts made.

The key is going to be with the in-coming Nigerian government is to rebuild the trust that was, for a variety of reasons, and there is blame, I think, on both sides, that was allowed to really disintegrate in the last year or year-and-a-half.

Mr. JOSCELYN. I think that is right. I think we have seen now, also, more regional cooperation with the government in Nigeria and the surrounding countries going after Boko Haram from different sides, and you can see Boko Haram is actually lashing out at other countries, like Chad and others, because of that. So there is definitely more regional cooperation there.

I just want to add one real quick thing to all this whole thing. There is another group in Nigeria that nobody talks about, which is called Ansaru, which is actually—it is al-Qaeda's front in Nigeria, and they are deliberately playing off of Boko Haram's excessive violence to try and inculcate its ideology in Nigeria.

So this is the way al-Qaeda's groups are basically playing off of and triangulating off of the Islamic State's presence. It is that type of thing which could lead to the next crisis somewhere down the line if they are actually successful with that type of effort.

Mr. HIGGINS. Well, let me just—what is that—what is the next crisis?

Mr. JOSCELYN. Well, see, here is the problem. What al-Qaeda is doing with these groups is that they are becoming—they are trying to portray themselves as a home-grown, local Nigerian effort. The problem is that they can commit acts of terror, they can do things that look like they are more part of the local community than being a foreign ISIS sort-of related sort-of effort. That becomes trickier to handle from a counterterrorism standpoint because then you are dealing with potentially a group that has much deeper roots in the community.

Now, this is a nascent effort. It is just getting underway. It is not something that is close to fruition, so I don't want to over-hype the threat. But it is just an important indication of what al-Qaeda is doing not just there but elsewhere, where they are actually actively triangulating off of ISIS's brutality to get more supporters.

Mr. BYMAN. Mr. Higgins, if I may, to add on the next crisis, one of the problems is that these groups are regional but often our response is not.

So we can have a success. Let's say somewhat miraculously things go well in Nigeria for the next few years. That doesn't mean these fighters all go away. Some of them will go to neighboring states.

So our success in one area can lead to failure, really, in another. Often bureaucratically and almost intellectually, we are not structured to handle this on a regional basis; we handle it country by country. That is something I think we should work on.

Mr. PHAM. If I may just add to your question on what is next, another—there are various groups throughout Africa, many of which have been active for some time with links. For example, in my written testimony I bring up the Allied Democratic Forces in the borderlands between Uganda and the Democratic Republic of the Congo.

It has existed for more than 20 years. Its leader, Jamil Mukulu has links to pre-9/11 al-Qaeda and terrorist groups in South Asia. It has been on a rampage for the last several months, several hundred people killed, including just last week 5 villagers who opposed them beheaded. It doesn't get any attention.

We have got other issues in the DRC and Uganda, so these are threats that are ignored but they are clearly on the uptick.

Mr. HIGGINS. Thank you.

Yield back, Mr. Chairman.

Mr. KING. Gentleman from Pennsylvania.

Mr. BARLETTA. Thank you, Mr. Chairman.

Dr. Pham, when we think of terrorism we often focus on the military response in dealing with it. What non-military initiatives should the United States be doing to try to combat and contain what is happening in Africa?

Mr. PHAM. Thank you very much, sir. Certainly we need to also ramp up not just support for partner militaries, but also policing and intelligence.

For example, Kenya has a relatively effective military. It has done very well helping us and other countries push Shabaab in Somalia. But the police service is a disaster. There were reporters who hopped into their cars who got to the Garissa University attack faster than the elite police unit, for want of transport.

So policing, and certainly these—although I adamantly push back against the idea that poverty makes people extremists, certainly underdevelopment, political, social, and economic marginalization presents a ready pool of potential people, and so the whole-government approach through some of these areas.

There is a reason why northeastern Nigeria was particularly susceptible to Boko Haram, and I can say that for many regions in Africa.

Mr. BARLETTA. Thank you.

Thank you, Mr. Chairman.

Mr. KING. We do have several more minutes. If I could just ask the question, and obviously then the Ranking Member can ask whatever questions he wants, so what European allies or what European countries do you feel could be more constructive or are being constructive now and, you know, which ones could be more constructive as far as coming up with a comprehensive, cohesive approach to terrorism in Africa?

Mr. JOSCELYN. Well, it is tough to say because each country in Africa, each part of Africa there are different probably pulls from different parts of Europe, so it is probably a different response for, say, like North Africa or Libya, where Italy is obviously the focus of our attention because they are the ones who are most proactive or not proactive in terms of combatting the threats; down to the French, when it comes to Mali and those sort of traditionally Thai areas.

You know, the bottom line, from my perspective, is that because everything is seen as ad hoc, as opposed to connected, there is no real grand strategy for combatting these groups as a whole. So basically, the strategy against ISIS in Libya could be one thing, whereas the strategy for the new ISIS-Boko Haram merger in Nigeria could be another thing.

In some cases there—obviously there are localized components of this whole thing, so that partly makes sense. But it doesn't make sense when you actually understand their strategy that is comprehensive, and it is across the, you know, large portions of the continent. AQIM is a great example of that, where they took advantage of the situation in Libya to basically overrun large portions of Mali by using the arms and a rear base.

So without that sort-of comprehensive look at the whole thing, and pooling resources, we should be—it should be an all-hands-on-deck effort, is what I am saying, where multiple European partnership should be involved with the United States and our African allies to basically look at it from that perspective.

Mr. KING. Are you saying, though, that basically unless a European country had a colonial interest in Africa it would have minimal influence today?

Mr. JOSCELYN. It is definitely tied in part to the colonial past, but there are more complicated issues, as well, in terms of current business interests when it comes to oil companies and others. But also, there are all sorts of potential reasons why European countries are invested in different parts of Africa.

Mr. KING. Dr. Pham.

Mr. PHAM. Mr. Chairman, in addition to Italy and France, as Mr. Joscelyn mentioned, I would also point out also that certainly our British friends are heavily invested, especially in West Africa and parts of East Africa.

Also, we shouldn't overlook our African partners. For example, Morocco has an extraordinary program on counter-radicalization. They are helping not only their own country, but also Tunisia, Mali, Guinea, with training of imams on more moderate forms of Islam, pushing back—a program pushing back radicalization. We signed a framework——

Mr. KING. If I could just say, we actually know very little about Morocco, so I am glad you brought that up today.

Mr. PHAM. We signed a framework agreement at the margins of the U.S.-Africa Leaders Summit last August with Morocco to partner with them, although the—on regional training. So that is an example, and certainly we can work with the African Union, especially the peace and security commissioner, who was just in town recently, again, seeking, actually, U.S. engagement. I had actually encouraged him to come back and come to the Hill and engage with—he had some very concrete—Ambassador Smail Chergui had some very concrete wish lists, and I think some of them were—dovetail very nicely with the concerns of this subcommittee and the committee.

Mr. KING. Dr. Byman.

Mr. BYMAN. I would only briefly add that a number of our allies, especially France, have shown a willingness to be quite active and to go into areas that are important but the United States has been reluctant to enter or engage with seriously, France and Mali being the great example.

We should be thinking fairly seriously about ways we can help their effort. It can be a lot of behind-the-scenes efforts; it can be intelligence, surveillance, and reconnaissance; it can be coordinating training efforts.

There is a lot that can be done where the Europeans are more logical countries to take the lead, and that is something we should see as a benefit rather than competition.

Mr. KING. Mr. Higgins.

Mr. HIGGINS. Yes. Thank you, Mr. Chairman.

The ISIS presence in the continent of Africa—is it likely to increase, I mean, their operations moving to the continent itself?

Mr. JOSCELYN. I will say this quickly: What Dr. Byman said earlier about it being tied to their military fortunes in Iraq and Syria is precisely correct, that basically as long as they can keep the caliphate claim going, that fuels recruitment in their sense of that they are this big sort of powerful entity that is taking on all comers. So that is a big part of it.

But in addition to that, they also have localized strategies for growing inside Libya and elsewhere across the continent. Really it is a complicated environment in each country. If you look at Libya it is a total mess. I mean, it is basically a seven- or eight-sided game right now inside Libya, which is hard to distill into one thing.

ISIS has inserted itself with a very simple message, that we are the caliphate and we are here. That has some advantages, but also has some disadvantages.

Mr. HIGGINS. So their—this strategy of ISIS is to be ever-present and to let that presence be known, because it is really all about control of territory. So their objective would be to control; is it conceivable that there could be an ISIS-al-Qaeda conflict?

Mr. JOSCELYN. Well, we have seen ISIS and al-Qaeda conflict across the board, including in Africa. In Libya, in fact, last summer, the local al-Qaeda group in Drerna actually killed the military commander for ISIS, shot him. There have been other sort-of instances like that, as well.

One quick thing: Al-Qaeda is also interested in controlling territory. They do control territory. They go about it very differently, which is—it is a whole—the end-game is very much the same, in terms of building a caliphate. Just that al-Qaeda has very different steps to get there.

Mr. HIGGINS. So this conflict between ISIS and al-Qaeda presumably will expand in the continent.

Mr. JOSCELYN. Yes. We have already seen indications of that. In fact, there were—there is actually—right now what is happening is that ISIS in Libya is taking on the Farj militia in Libya and other Islamist groups in Libya. In some cases they are running into al-Qaeda pushback as well; in some cases they are cooperating with al-Qaeda fronts in Libya. So it is complicated.

Mr. HIGGINS. Where is Abu Bakr al-Baghdadi today?

Mr. JOSCELYN. There are reports that he is injured. I don't know that that is true. We see reports that he has a severe spinal cord injury all the way to the idea that he is dead.

I don't know how much of those are true at this point. We have seen an official denial by some people in the U.S. Government. I basically leave that very open-ended.

Mr. HIGGINS. Yield back.

Mr. KING. Lou, do you have any questions?

Okay. Let me thank the witnesses for your testimony. We have just been notified the votes are coming up in a matter of minutes, but I want to thank you for your testimony today.

I want to thank the Members for their questions, thank the Ranking Member for his cooperation.

Our Members of the subcommittee may have additional questions, and we will ask you to respond to those in writing. With that, pursuant to committee rule 7(e), the hearing record will be held open for 10 days.

Without objection, the subcommittee stands adjourned. Again, thank you very much.

[Whereupon, at 1:33 p.m., the subcommittee was adjourned.]